The Future of North American Integration

THE FUTURE OF NORTH AMERICAN INTEGRATION

Beyond NAFTA

PETER HAKIM

and

ROBERT E. LITAN

editors

BROOKINGS INSTITUTION PRESS
Washington, D.C.

Copyright © 2002
THE BROOKINGS INSTITUTION
1775 Massachusetts Avenue, N.W., Washington, D.C. 20036
www.brookings.edu

Library of Congress Cataloging-in-Publication data

The future of North American integration : beyond NAFTA /
Peter Hakim and Robert E. Litan, editors
p. cm.
Includes bibliographical references and index.
ISBN 0-8157-3398-4 (cloth : alk. paper)
ISBN 0-8157-3399-2 (pbk. : alk. paper)
1. Free trade—North America. 2. Canada. Treaties, etc.
3. North America—Economic integration. I. Hakim, Peter.
II. Litan, Robert E., 1950–
HF1746.F87 2002   2002009133
337.1'7—dc21

9 8 7 6 5 4 3 2 1

The paper used in this publication meets minimum
requirements of the American National Standard for
Information Sciences—Permanence of Paper for
Printed Library Materials: ANSI Z39.48-1992.

Typeset in Palatino

Composition by Stephen D. McDougal
Mechanicsville, Maryland

Printed by R. R. Donnelley and Sons
Harrisonburg, Virginia

FOREWORD

"Integration" has a powerful and positive resonance in the vocabulary of American policy and politics. The word is associated with progress, fairness, mutual benefit, good governance, and a healthy community. But for some, it's been a fighting word, associated with take-no-prisoners debate and even violence. That's because what one person, or one part of the community, advocates as a welcome step, others resist as a threat to their status, well-being, security, and even their freedom.

Starting in the 1950s, integration referred most commonly to the mammoth task of breaking down discriminatory barriers between the races in U.S. laws, the educational system, and social structures. While that effort continues, in recent years integration has, like so many other words, taken on connotations pertaining to international life. Specifically, it refers to the process whereby states open their borders, societies, cultures, and economies, building common institutions on the basis of common values and interests.

The most advanced example of integration is on the far side of the Atlantic. Fifteen nation-states that spent much of the three and a half centuries since the Peace of Westphalia making war against each other have pooled significant aspects of their sovereignty under the blue and gold-starred flag of the European Union.

In the Western Hemisphere, there are similar ventures under way, though at earlier stages of development. Mercosur/Mercosul began as a common market among Argentina, Brazil, and Chile, but in the nineties it took on some political and diplomatic functions as well. Similarly, the Andean Pact has been expanded to create a broader political and economic structure including Bolivia, Colombia, Ecuador, Peru, and Venezuela.

One factor impeding integration in this hemisphere is the sheer predominance of the United States. Integration requires a degree of equality among its participants, otherwise it can become a euphemism for hegemony. Another factor is the deep and enduring strain of skepticism in the American body politic about any infringement on sovereignty.

Nonetheless, as early as the 1980s, many (though not all) political leaders and citizens of the United States began to recognize the imperative of reconciling American independence with global interdependence. The obvious place to start was in our own neighborhood—the Americas.

The most dramatic result is North American integration, which is stitching more closely together the United States, Canada, and Mexico. That is the subject of this book, which my colleague, Robert Litan, vice president and director of our Economic Studies department, and Peter Hakim have assembled from the proceedings of a conference at Brookings in December 2001.

The North American Free Trade Agreement, or NAFTA, is perhaps the most conspicuous—and controversial—manifestation of the process. The idea for NAFTA originated in Mexico, when then-president Carlos Salinas wanted to lock in the market-oriented reforms he had introduced. The agreement subsequently won bipartisan support in the United States—including from Presidents George Bush and William Clinton. At the same time, because it envisioned a special trade and investment relationship with Mexico, a country that was much less economically developed than the United States, NAFTA aroused fears among many Americans that the agreement could threaten their jobs. Indeed, it required Vice President Al Gore to debate Ross Perot and rebut the charge that NAFTA would produce a "giant sucking sound" of jobs going to Mexico (a fear that did not materialize). The U.S. House of Representatives barely passed the agreement in 1993.

Ironically, as Bob, Peter, and the other authors of this volume make clear, linkages between the three countries were growing, and arousing passions, well before NAFTA. Furthermore, integration has not only accelerated since the agreement became effective, it also is evident in areas well beyond the purview of NAFTA itself.

A key question, at the center of this book, is the future of North American integration. Will it, and should it, continue on its own, without further encouragement from governments? Or should governments build on NAFTA and improve coordination on a wide range of matters extending beyond trade and investment, such as immigration, energy, transportation, law enforcement, counter-terrorism, and security?

In the pages that follow, experts from the three NAFTA countries—all participants in the December 2001 conference—tackle these questions forcefully and clearly. That gathering was cosponsored by a number of other organizations: the Inter-American Dialogue (which Peter has led with great distinction for eight years); the Mexican Council on Foreign Relations (CMRI); the National Policy Association; the Policy Research Initiative of the Canadian Government; the Conference Board of Canada; the Public Policy Forum of Canada; and the Technological Institute of Mexico (ITAM). We at Brookings thank our partners in those organizations.

Foreword

Bob and Peter are also grateful for the editorial assistance of Colleen McGuiness; secretarial and organizational assistance provided by Alicia Jones; verification of factual material in the manuscript by Catherine Theohary; and research assistance by Sandip Sukhtankar. This project was funded by a grant from the Canadian government and by funds provided by Brookings.

All of us hope that this volume will help inform the public and frame constructive debate in the years to come as North American integration goes forward.

Strobe Talbott
President

Washington, D.C.
September 2002

CONTENTS

1

INTRODUCTION

PETER HAKIM AND ROBERT E. LITAN

When it came into force on January 1, 1994, the North
American Free Trade Agreement (NAFTA) joined the economic futures of Canada, Mexico, and the United States.
Clearly both Canada and Mexico—given their geography
and markets—had been integrating with the United States
well before NAFTA took effect. Indeed, the United States
and Canada had signed a bilateral free trade accord six
years earlier. But, with NAFTA in place, the pace of integration accelerated, and systematic rules governing trade
and investment along with dispute resolution mechanisms
were established, and the governments assumed an active
role in guiding, promoting, and managing economic relations among the three countries. Moreover, the three countries are increasingly viewed as a single economic entity,
one with a gross domestic product (GDP) of some $10 tril-

1

lion, or 15 percent larger than the fifteen-country European Union (EU).

What then lies ahead for North America? As it stands, NAFTA takes a narrow view of integration, focusing almost exclusively on trade and investment matters, steering clear of any new institutional, social, or development arrangements. NAFTA barely addresses such vital issues as immigration policy and labor markets, the energy sector, environmental protection, and law enforcement. Moreover, despite their trilateral relationship, the three governments of North America largely conduct business within the framework of two bilateral relationships, that is, between Canada and the United States and between Mexico and the United States.

The governments of Canada, Mexico, and the United States now must confront the question of whether NAFTA is enough. Do they want to keep their trilateral relationship largely focused on economic matters? Or are they interested in integrating more deeply, in more fully joining their societies—perhaps initiating a process to build a North American Community, if not precisely along the lines of the European Union, then something similar but less ambitious? Whatever the three countries decide their ultimate objective to be, what additional steps, if any, should they take in the interim to affect the pace and structure of their integration?

This monograph is designed to begin a process to help answer these questions. It contains thoughtful discussions about the future of North America by three knowledgeable experts on the continent from each of the three countries. Robert A. Pastor from American University (and formerly with Emory University) in the United States has written a comprehensive book on the subject: *Toward a North American Community: Lessons from the Old World for the New*.[1] Andrés Rozental is an ambassador at large for Mexico and president of Consejo Mexicano de Asuntos Internacionales (Mexican Council on International Affairs). Perrin Beatty, a former foreign minister of Canada, is president and chief executive officer of Canadian Manufacturers & Exporters.

The papers in this volume were presented at a conference held at the Brookings Institution in December 2001, as part of a project on the future of North American integration. The project has the support of eight organizations from the three North American countries.[2] The consortium was formed to explore the issues and choices that lie ahead—including the costs, benefits, and constraints associated with various options—as the three nations consider the kind of future relationship they wish to develop. The project seeks to assist decisionmakers, opinion leaders, and ordinary citizens in understanding the promise and challenges associated with the integration of Canada, Mexico, and the United

States. It also aims to encourage them to think more systematically about how they wish to proceed and where they want to end up.

North American Economic Integration

The United States in 2002 is overwhelmingly the largest trading partner of both Canada and Mexico and the biggest foreign investor in both countries.

Total trade between the United States and Canada amounts to about $450 billion per year, nearly two-and-one-half times what it was in the early 1990s. Canada buys some 70 percent of its imports from U.S. suppliers and sends more than 85 percent of its exports to the U.S. market. Nearly two-thirds of all foreign investment comes from the United States.

Trade between the United States and Mexico exceeds $250 billion per year, more than four times that of a decade ago. Mexico ships almost 90 percent of it exports to the United States and obtains about 70 percent of its imports from the United States. Mexico has become the second largest trading partner of the United States, and if the growth of its bilateral commerce continues at its current rate, Mexico could soon be challenging Canada's no. 1 ranking. Mexican exports to the United States, once largely made up of petroleum and agricultural products, are now more than 85 percent manufactured goods.

Although it does not come anywhere close to the amount of either country's bilateral commerce with the United States, trade between Canada and Mexico increased nearly fivefold in the past ten years. The two countries are now each others' third largest trading partner—trailing only the United States and the EU. The amount they sell to and buy from each other amounts to some $9 billion, nearly as much as the trade between Brazil and Argentina.

Economic integration among the three countries already goes considerably beyond trade and investment. Mexicans continue to migrate in large numbers to the United States, principally in search of jobs and higher wages. Upwards of 21 million persons of Mexican origin now reside in the United States. Approximately 9 million of these were born in Mexico. They contribute in countless ways to the U.S. economy and society.

Mexicans and Mexican Americans now send some $8 billion annually back to their communities. Although the numbers are still modest, a growing number of Mexicans are also finding their way to Canada. And tourism is expanding in all three countries, or at least it was before the September 11, 2001, terrorist attacks on the United States.

The three countries are tied together in many noneconomic ways as well. Mexicans are changing language patterns, social norms, and culture throughout the United States. As Mexican migrants become residents and citizens, they are increasingly influencing local and national politics. The voting strength and preferences of Mexican Americans are shaping U.S. policy toward Mexico. At the same time, U.S. cultural phenomena are increasingly pervasive in both Mexico and Canada—through films, TV, music, tourists, and student and professional exchanges. Nongovernmental organizations of many types function easily across the borders of all three countries.

The Future of North American Integration

Unless the three governments decide to halt further integration, recent trends strongly suggest that the societies and economies of the United States, Canada, and Mexico are likely to draw closer together. In particular, cross-border trade, investment, and migration should all continue to increase.

Stronger cooperation is clearly the aim of the three governments. That was made plain in the joint statement of U.S. president George W. Bush, Mexican president Vicente Fox, and Canadian prime minister Jean Chrétien issued in April 2001 during the Quebec City Summit of the Americas. The three leaders recognized that "patterns of cooperation—by governments, business, and other members of civil society—are building a new sense of community among us." And they pledged to "work to deepen a sense of community, promote our mutual economic interest, and ensure that NAFTA's benefits extend to all regions and social sectors." To achieve this objective, the three leaders called for "coordinating efforts in support of efficient North American energy markets" and strengthening "trilateral cooperation to address the legitimate needs of migrants," while pledging to "examine options to further strengthen our North American partnership . . . and advance the trilateral relationship."

President Fox, since his election in July 2000, has most energetically pursued the goal of North American integration. Even before taking office in December 2000, he traveled to Ottawa and Washington, with several groundbreaking proposals for strengthening ties among the three countries. He called on his U.S. and Canadian counterparts to consider transforming NAFTA from a free trade arrangement to a common market and to work toward the goal of open borders, for people as well as goods, among the three countries. Although largely rebuffed on these ambitious aims, Fox has continued to press for deeper integration among all three countries particularly focused, unsurprisingly, on Mexico's bilateral relationship with the United States.

Introduction

President Bush and many members of the U.S. Congress, even those with a history of antagonism toward Mexico, have endorsed the idea of reshaping U.S. policy toward Mexico in such sensitive areas as immigration and drugs and in pursuing closer economic ties. Bush has called the U.S. relationship with Mexico its most important in the world.

The events of September 11 radically transformed the foreign policy agenda of the United States—and shifted priorities in U.S. relations with Mexico and Canada. Border security commanded most of the immediate attention of policymakers in the United States, while the issues of greatest concern to Mexico and Canada—resolving outstanding trade disputes and reshaping immigration policies, the core issues of any integration effort—appeared to lose their urgency. Instead, security matters became a central focus for collaboration among the three governments. Canada and Mexico recognized the importance of security concerns on their own merits, but they were also intensely aware that, in light of changed U.S. priorities, security cooperation was essential to sustain normal cross-border commerce, capital flows, and the movement of people. The agendas of the three countries may be less congruent than they were before September 11, but the three countries each now have different, and possibly stronger, reasons for integration.

INTRODUCTION

Different Paths toward Integration

Although many political leaders in the United States, Canada, and Mexico agree that greater economic and political coordination among the three countries would be desirable, no preferred formula or path for achieving that coordination has yet emerged. Wide differences exist on how to proceed, depending on a range of factors, including specific interests at stake, ideological preferences, and pragmatic judgments of what is possible.

Fully Implement NAFTA

For those supportive of further integration—and all of the authors in this volume are to varying degrees—it is crucial that, at a minimum, NAFTA be fully implemented. So far, the provisions of the accord have been largely fulfilled on schedule, but a great deal still needs to be done to meet its requirements in both letter and spirit.

In particular, many in Mexico have expressed concern about U.S. compliance with NAFTA on issues as varied as sugar and trucking. For their part, Canadians were irritated about the recent imposition of U.S. tariffs on its lumber exports and concerned about possible new barriers raised against the import of Canadian wheat and steel. While all of these matters may not be specifically covered by NAFTA, many in Canada feel that the United States is not showing good faith by restricting free trade in key commodities. As for the United States, many policymakers and citizens remain concerned about Mexico's adherence to NAFTA's rules of origin provisions and its labor and environmental side agreements.

Some advocates of closer North American links argue that, for the next several years, the three governments ought to focus only on resolving these various disputes and work to ensure the full implementation of NAFTA. Several arguments are cited to support this view.

For one thing, NAFTA provides the core legal and institutional framework for integration. If it cannot be made to work, then how can the governments think of further initiatives to deepen integration? Pursuing other integration strategies could end up weakening the commitment to NAFTA and defer its completion.

Moreover, some dark clouds on the horizon could make NAFTA even more difficult to implement in the years ahead as the scheduled tariff reductions under the agreement become more binding, especially in Mexico. Facing greater competition from the north, domestic constituencies within Mexico may resist full implementation of NAFTA. These pressures are likely to grow if the United States is not seen as adhering to its part of the agreement. A similar backlash could arise in Canada if the future trade disputes emerge over issues other than the export of Canadian lumber and wheat to the United States. (A possible trade conflict with Canada and Mexico over steel was muted when the Bush administration decided in March 2001 to exempt exports from those countries from the safeguard tariffs it imposed on steel imported from most other countries.)

One suggestion for minimizing future conflict over NAFTA-related issues, advocated by Robert Pastor, might be to establish a permanent North American Court on Trade and Investment, which would replace the current ad hoc tribunals provided for under the agreement. The rulings of this court would be binding, as is the case now for the ad hoc tribunals. In addition, a permanent court could avoid the conflicts of interest that are becoming prevalent because of the difficulty of finding judges on a temporary basis, and it would permit the accumulation of precedent and thus the development of a more stable framework for trade and investment. The court's proceedings should be transparent: Its hearings should be open to the public, and opportunities should exist for interested parties from all countries to present briefs on disputes that come before the tribunal.

Moving beyond NAFTA

Designing and implementing additional integration measures beyond NAFTA will be difficult, if not impossible, until policymakers and citizens reach broad agreement on medium- and longer-run objectives. The effort will be complicated by the fragmentation inherent in the political systems of all three countries—embodied in separation of powers between different branches of government at the national level and in federalism between national and provincial or state governments. Three possible broad paths toward greater integration show the long-run choices with respect to integration that each nation confronts.

1. A NAFTA-plus arrangement would be limited to additional trade and investment measures that might lead to a full-fledged customs union with a common external tariff.

2. Deeper integration would seek accords on other subjects in which there are cross-border impacts, including migration, energy and water management, transportation and infrastructure, security arrangements, and foreign policy consultations.

3. A supranational institutions option could involve modest arrangements to deal with specific issues or sectors, or it could be as ambitious as entailing EU-style intergovernmental executive and legislative functions.

These are not mutually exclusive paths. Leaders and citizens of the three countries could agree on an eclectic policy framework that contains elements of each of these broad models.

INTRODUCTION

NAFTA-Plus

A NAFTA-plus arrangement would build on NAFTA, but the focus of any new integration effort would be kept on trade and investment. This approach, for example, might turn NAFTA from a free trade agreement into a full-fledged customs union with a common external tariff. Over the longer run, it could also contemplate the strengthening and deepening of economic coordination generally—for instance, through increased harmonization of regulations and macroeconomic policy. Policy harmonization might eventually aim toward a common currency (although a consensus at the December Brookings meeting was that talk of a common currency is premature and that flexible exchange rates so far have worked relatively well to smooth out each country's adjustments to macroeconomic shocks).

Other nontrade measures could also facilitate trade. One example would be an integrated continental plan for improving transportation between the three countries by, among other things, establishing common vehicle safety standards and eliminating restrictions against domestic carriage by foreign providers (airlines in particular). If appropriate security measures could be agreed upon, a North American open-skies arrangement could be contemplated. The many different subnational and national transportation regulatory standards make harmonization an extremely ambitious goal, however. Seeking the adoption of minimal standards coupled with mutual recognition of standards across countries (an approach to standards adopted by the EU) might be more feasible.

Consideration could also be given to widening—instead of deepening—NAFTA to incorporate other neighboring countries such as those of Central America and the Caribbean. President Bush has endorsed such an option by announcing his intention to begin negotiations for a free trade arrangement with the Central American and Caribbean region. In addition, Canada and Mexico already have bilateral agreements with many of the countries in the two regions. Some argue, however, that widening NAFTA to include these additional countries may weaken the original agreement and detract from the potentially larger benefits of achieving deeper integration among just the three NAFTA partners.

Deeper Integration

Another direction for integration would be to develop more formal cooperative arrangements in other critical areas outside trade and investment. The most important of these would be security, migration, and labor movement. Others might include energy and water management, infrastructure development, and even foreign policy.

The events following September 11 pushed the United States to cooperate more closely with both Canada and Mexico in border management. Both countries have agreed to expand efforts to check trucks and other vehicles destined for the United States. Various participants at the December Brookings conference suggested the countries take more ambitious steps, ranging from further improvements in coordination of customs and immigration procedures of the three countries to a merger of these functions into a single North American Customs and Immigration Service.

The terrorist attacks had the opposite effect, at least so far, on migration issues. Just before those events, the United States seemed open to considering a major guest worker program for Mexican citizens. The momentum behind that idea has since cooled, but the problems posed by illegal immigration from Mexico to the United States will not go away. The participants at the December conference did not explicitly discuss how to move forward from here.

While energy trade is vigorous among the three countries, various impediments stand in the way of any expansion. The Mexican government, for example, imposes high taxes on Pemex, its state-owned oil company, to meet its revenue requirements. This policy discourages investment in the country's oil sector. The idea that Pemex be privatized remains a politically charged issue in Mexico. Canadian governments, federal and provincial, maintain some controls over the export of electricity and water. Meanwhile, from the Canadian and Mexican perspective, the United States lacks a well-defined national energy policy. Given these constraints, the short-run prospects of removing impediments to energy and resource trade between the countries are slim—even as a tripartite working group has been meeting to discuss national and subnational policies on energy.

EU-Style Supranational Institutions

The most ambitious approach would be to adopt something like the EU model. The notion of an EU-style arrangement for North America—in which some governmental functions are devolved to a regional authority—seems politically unrealistic at the present time when even NAFTA remains controversial. Moreover, there are many differences between the EU and North America. The major members in the EU are more equal in size, whereas NAFTA is defined by its asymmetry. The members of the EU were driven to form a regional framework in large part as a way to secure peace on the continent. While the United States fought Canada and Mexico in the early part of the nineteenth century, the borders have been peaceful for more than one hundred years, and the incentives for integration have been primarily economic.

Nonetheless, the EU's fifty years of experience integrating fifteen diverse countries may provide some lessons and ideas that could be relevant to a different North American model. The EU experience might serve as a useful framework for political leaders and citizens in all three countries as they consider the depth and nature of further integration efforts. In some sense, the North American region is already more integrated than the EU. Despite the freedom of movement across European borders contemplated by the Schengen agreement, cross-border movement—especially out-migration from the poorer countries (Greece, Portugal, and Spain) to the richer countries in the EU—so far has been surprisingly small. Some analysts believe this is one of the consequences of a very successful cohesion policy by the EU that has narrowed the disparities between rich and poor countries. If migration between Mexico and the United States is to be reduced, similar policies may be needed.

Building North American Institutions

As of the spring of 2002, no strong consensus had emerged in the three nations—reflected as well as during the December 2001 conference held at Brookings—for NAFTA-plus, deeper integration, or supranational institutions. Nonetheless, the interests of citizens of all three countries would be served by launching more systematic processes aimed at developing some measure of consensus around a longer-term vision of a North American project. This is especially important because, notwithstanding NAFTA, the primary focus of each country has been on its bilateral relationships with the other two countries. Trilateral institutions are weak, and they are largely limited to NAFTA commissions and dispute resolution panels. Several ideas for strengthening trilateral institutions were discussed at the December conference, but it was recognized that the role and characteristics of any new institutions will depend on how much the countries want to accelerate integration efforts and their common vision of how those efforts should proceed.

Robert Pastor suggests that the governments should establish a new North American Commission that, on an ongoing basis, would seek input from citizens, experts, and opinion leaders in the three countries and provide advice to the three national governments—and possibly certain state and provincial governments—about the preparation and implementation of a "North American agenda."[3] Such an agenda could include but is not limited to the following policy subjects: trade and investment, infrastructure development, security and immigration cooperation, and further integration of resource trade among the countries. The commission could provide its advice either informally or at semi-annual or annual summits of leaders of the three countries.

A related proposal that Pastor advances would be to transform the two existing legislative consultative groups, U.S.-

Mexican and U.S.-Canadian, into a North American Parliamentary Group. This group would provide a significant forum for legislators from the three countries to exchange views regularly on issues of common interest. There may be benefits as well to providing a more formal structure to the ongoing meetings of governors and premiers from the border states.

Whether or not these intergovernmental consultative mechanisms are established, more exchanges of experts and citizens should occur between the three countries. These efforts could generate ideas that ultimately affect public attitudes and government policies in the three countries. More such efforts should be encouraged, perhaps aimed at fleshing out integration proposals for specific sectors or policy initiatives.

Pursuing Integration

The experience of NAFTA suggests that all three countries have gained economically from the expansion in trade and investment. This suggests that further integration will contribute to rising incomes and productivity in the three nations. At the same time, deeper integration—especially that entailing some degree of shared governance—challenges traditional notions of sovereignty. Moreover, to the degree that further integration involves additional competitive challenges to certain industries or groups in the three countries—low-skilled American workers, for example—it is likely to arouse political opposition even in the best of circumstances.

For all these reasons, the benefits and costs of further integration need to be weighed against each other, and their impacts on different groups within each of the societies assessed carefully. Additional steps toward integration beyond the closer ties that are likely to deepen naturally, while they may be mutually beneficial, must be managed and explained to the peoples of the countries to gain support.

Mexico has the greatest stake in building closer and denser economic ties because, in per capita terms, its economy lags so substantially behind those of Canada and the United States. The huge size of the U.S. and Canadian economies, combined more than twenty times that of the Mexican economy, provides a continually expanding demand for Mexican products and a ready source of investment capital for the country—all of which should accelerate Mexico's growth prospects and help it converge toward Canadian and U.S. income levels. In turn, an economically thriving Mexico serves important U.S. and Canadian interests. Economic development in Mexico will contribute to stability and democracy within the country, making it more attractive for foreign direct investment and an expanding market for exports from both northern neighbors.

The United States, Mexico, and Canada also should all gain from an integration strategy that leads to the more effective management of migration issues, which may be the source of the greatest tension between Mexico and its two northern neighbors. Ironically, past U.S.-Mexican migration created the cultural and social roots for greater integration between the two countries. That migration has also increased the political motivation in the United States for integration with Mexico in particular, as the number of Mexican American voters steadfastly expands and they gain expanding political influence.

All three countries also are in a position to gain from more systematic collaboration in dealing with a range of other problems, including criminal drug trafficking, environmental protection, energy and water management, and transportation, communications, and other infrastructure development.

Hard Decisions and Hard Work Ahead

There is no easy path to greater integration for the three nations of North America. In each country, sizable groups, perhaps even majorities, remain unhappy about NAFTA and its results, and substantial political resistance exists to further integration from those who are convinced they will lose more than they will gain. They include workers who are afraid of losing their jobs, firms fearing competition or worried about having to sell out to foreign owners, politicians and citizens who are concerned about diminished sovereign authority, and groups that worry about changes in social policies and institutions and the dilution of national cultures.

The main roadblock to integration, however, is the huge disparity in income and wealth between Mexico and its two NAFTA partners. Mexico's per capita income is roughly one-sixth of that of the United States and a quarter of that of Canada. Living standards—measured by wages, education levels, housing quality, health statistics, mortality rates, and public services of all kinds—reflect these enormous differences, which are far greater than ever existed between any two members of the EU. Meanwhile, the difference in per capita income between the United States and Canada has widened considerably in the past decade, as the U.S. per capita GDP grew by more than 50 percent and Canada's growth was less than 10 percent. The U.S.-Canadian income gap is large by European standards, but it does not appear to be a major impediment to enhanced integration, in part because Canada continues to perform better on a number of key quality of life indicators. A growing productivity differential between the two nations may be more of an obstacle.

In addition, the sharp income and wealth differences between Mexico and its northern neighbors cannot be ignored, because they interfere directly with the solution of so many shared problems. The most important of these are migration and labor flows, which are largely driven by wage differentials and cannot be controlled without sharply diminishing the gap. As long as the wage difference is so massive, it will be difficult ever to shake American and Canadian workers of their belief that industries and jobs will consistently move toward Mexico in search of cheap labor—the core of their opposition to NAFTA and its expansion. Moreover, along with other poor countries, Mexico confronts serious problems of corruption, which make cooperation in antidrug campaigns and other law enforcement efforts difficult. Even without corruption, Mexico would lack the resources to be a good partner in combating terrorism, drugs, or environmental deterioration, among other common threats.

There is no simple or rapid way to reduce the income gap. Mexico simply has to expand its economy at a significantly faster rate than either the United States or Canada. Even if the Mexican economy were to grow 3 percent a year faster than either of its NAFTA partners, the country would need more than twenty years to reach one-half of Canada's GDP per capita and more than thirty years to attain one-half of the United States' GDP per capita.

But the long-term nature of the project should not be an excuse for pessimism. Just one generation ago, the nations of Southeast Asia were among the poorest in the world. Today, many residents in that region enjoy living standards that will soon approach those of developed economies.

The pace at which the income gap between Mexico and its northern neighbors will narrow is mainly up to the policymakers and citizens of Mexico, who will have to sustain appropriate fiscally disciplined, growth-oriented policies; maintain the confidence of external investors; complete their economic reform agenda; and invest substantial domestic resources in infrastructure and human capital.

The United States and Canada, however, will also have to decide how much, if anything, they are prepared to do to help bridge the income gap between themselves and Mexico. The World Bank, for example, estimates that Mexico will need in the coming decade $20 billion more financing for infrastructure development than it is likely to secure from currently available sources, public or private.[4]

Where could such additional monies come from? One possibility is a new fund managed by the World Bank or Inter-American Development Bank or both. Another idea is to enlarge the North American Development Bank, which could raise funds on the capital markets based on pledges from the United States and Canada. The Andean Development Corporation also has shown the productive contribution a regional development bank can make. Although all five of its core member countries are poorer than Mexico (let alone the United States or Canada), the Andean Development Corporation has been consistently able to secure private capital at investment-grade interest rates. A North American bank should be able to do as well.

A considerable difference of opinion exists, however, about the potential efficacy and political feasibility of having the two richer partners transfer substantial resources to Mexico in the mold of the social cohesion funds of the EU. The gap between the richer and poorer countries in the EU has been significantly reduced in the last decades, but views differ as to the exact contribution of the EU's social cohesion funds, as opposed to private investment and freer trade.

In addition to the economic gap, Mexico's institutional problems make its integration with the United States and Canada more difficult. For ordinary U.S. and Canadian citizens and their representatives in Washington and Ottawa, Mexico is a less desirable partner because of corruption, as well as the shortcomings of its justice and law enforcement systems. The election of Vicente Fox, the first opposition candidate to take power peacefully in Mexico's history, demonstrated Mexico's important progress toward democracy—and was widely welcomed in the United States and Canada. As part of the effort to promote North American integration, Mexico, however, still needs to meet the continuing challenge of strengthening its democratic institutions and become a more open and just society.

All three countries also will have to confront issues of sovereignty and basic nationalism in deciding how much more integration to pursue. Virtually by definition, multilateral cooperation leads to the loss of sovereign decisionmaking power. In exchange for expected benefits, NAFTA has required the United States, Mexico, and Canada to substitute mutually agreed upon rules and joint dispute resolution procedures for what had previously been national decisions. Deeper North American integration will introduce more common rules and regulations, more joint decisionmaking, and perhaps even new trilateral institutions. These changes will provoke opposition among groups in all three countries that will use traditional conceptions of sovereignty as their defense.

At first blush, it would seem that Canada and Mexico—because they are smaller and less powerful—would gain most from the development of joint procedures, rules, and institutions, which could restrain the more powerful United States and make it harder for the United States to get its own way. However, the two smaller nations are concerned on at least two counts. First, the United States, because of its size and power, may dominate any trilateral arrangements that are established. Second, even if such arrangements do help restrain the United States, further integration itself will lead to U.S. dominance. Canadians in particular also are worried about the dilution of their culture and the potential that their country's safety nets and other social policies will inevitably be watered down. Mexicans, for their part, worry about increasing U.S. control of their industries, displacing important elements of their culture, and American corporations taking command of the nation's natural resources.

Another key challenge that all three countries must confront as they consider further steps toward integration is how to avoid weakening ongoing global and regional trade negotiations, including the new World Trade Organization (WTO) round and the Free Trade Area of the Americas (FTAA). The political energy devoted to cementing a North American arrangement may divert attention from these broader initiatives. Yet, by pursuing a deeper North American agenda, all three countries might be able to develop a common front in such negotiations, thus enhancing their bargaining leverage.

Finally, whatever efforts are made to join their economies together, all three countries will become even more vulnerable to the economic decisions and performances of their partners. A booming economy in one nation will enhance economic prospects in the others. Similarly, the consequences of an economic recession or crisis will be transmitted across an integrated North America. Mexico and Canada are far more vulnerable to U.S. economic vicissitudes than vice versa. After all, the economy of Mexico is one-twentieth and the economy of Canada is one-tenth the size of the economy of the United States, and both are heavily reliant on trade with and investment from the United States. But they will also benefit a good deal more from a prospering United States than the United States will gain from a prospering Canada or Mexico.

Conclusion

Even if the three governments take no further steps, the economies, societies, cultures, and institutions of three countries should continue to integrate on their own accord. The three countries now face a decision of whether and how they should seek to accelerate, smooth, and institutionalize this integration process. This will not be a simple challenge. Much more dialogue between the three governments and their citizens will be required to reach consensus on the broad goals and specific policies that any such further integration may entail. The major objective of this volume and of the North American project is to begin this dialogue and the search for ways to develop "win-win-win" strategies for all three countries and their citizens.

Notes

1. Robert A. Pastor, *Toward a North American Community: Lessons from the Old World for the New* (Washington: Institute for International Economics, 2001).

2. The organizations are the Brookings Institution, Inter-American Dialogue, Mexican Council on Foreign Relations, National Policy Association, Policy Research Initiative of the Canadian Government, the Conference Board of Canada, Public Policy Forum of Canada, and Technological Institute of Mexico.

3. Pastor, *Toward a North American Community*.

4. In addition, some efficiencies could be realized from the existing infrastructure system through such marketlike devices as congestion pricing.

2

CANADA IN NORTH AMERICA
Isolation or Integration?

PERRIN BEATTY

Even before Confederation, Canadians' views of themselves were shaped and defined by their relationship with their southern neighbors.

Canada was born of the fear that, without banding together, the remaining colonies of British North America would inexorably be absorbed by the stronger and more populous nation to the south. More than forty thousand American loyalists had migrated north after the War of Independence, determined to live under British institutions and laws, and their influence on Canadian opinion remained strong. The War of 1812–14 had underscored the profound

The author is grateful for advice provided by the staff of Canadian Manufacturers & Exporters (CME). The opinions presented, however, are those of the author and should not be considered CME policy.

differences between the peoples on the two sides of the border, and the American notion of manifest destiny to absorb the colonies left Canadians little reason for complacency.

Tensions between the two peoples remained high throughout the second half of the nineteenth century. President Abraham Lincoln imposed for the first time the requirement for passports for Canadians entering the United States, and the U.S. administration felt that Canadians had tilted in favor of the South during the Civil War. For their part, the British colonies found themselves attacked by Fenian raiders based on American soil.

The end of reciprocity in 1866 threatened Canada's fragile industrial base. Coupled with political deadlock in the legislature, it encouraged Canadian statesman John A. Macdonald to propose that the maritime colonies unite with Canada East and West in a confederation that might ensure their independence. Macdonald's political platform advocated the extension of Canada's boundaries horizontally along the American border, linking the territory by rail, and the establishment of tariff barriers to protect the domestic market for Canadian manufacturers.

In the years that followed, the struggle to define and strengthen Canada's nationhood has been a key thread running though the country's history. Successive Canadian governments have acted to safeguard Canadian independence, which they considered threatened by the continentalist pull of economics. The Canadian Broadcasting Corporation, the country's public broadcaster, extended radio beyond the major centers and responded to fears that private broadcasters would affiliate with American networks. The Trans-Canada Highway provided travelers with a modern roadway across Canada. In the 1960s, Canadian broadcasting quotas mandated increased domestic content and the government created the Foreign Investment Review Agency to screen foreign (mostly American) investment in Canada. Only after the Progressive Conservative government came to office in 1984 was the agency abolished.

Despite government's efforts, geography, culture, technology, and trade draw Canada toward the United States. Canadian writers may nurture a romantic vision of a northern people with unique values and experiences contrasting with those of their American neighbors, but globalization in Canada wears a distinctly American face.

Almost nine in every ten Canadians lives within a hundred miles of the U.S. border. Even where American television networks are not available directly off air, they are distributed to all parts of Canada by cable and by satellite. Canadian newsstands are filled with American titles, and Canadians and Americans build and drive the same cars, drink coffee at Starbucks, and buy their children's clothes at the Gap. They share the defense of North America through the North American Aerospace Defense Command

(NORAD) and have fought alongside each other in war. They have the same technical standards for telephony, broadcasting, transportation, and electricity. They speak English with similar accents and idioms, and Canadian cities double for New York or Chicago in American movies. Canadians and Americans vacation together, work together, and trade together. They have created cooperative institutions such as the International Joint Commission on the Great Lakes, established in 1909 to help regulate the waterways between the two countries. Crossing between the two countries has been relatively easy for over a century, and advances in transportation and communications technology have overcome the barriers of distance. In addition, the values that animate both societies—democracy, free enterprise, individual rights, freedom of speech and religion—are similar.

Viewed from the United States, the relationship seems positive, if sometimes little more exciting than contemplating the insulation in the attic. U.S. politicians focus their efforts on advancing American strategic interests in areas where they are threatened or where other significant bilateral concerns exist. When issues arise with Canada, they are more likely to be considered irritants than fundamental problems, leading Washington, D.C., to take relations with Canada for granted. This American benign neglect sometimes raises concern for Canadian governments that oscillate between fear that Canada will receive too much attention from the United States and worry that it will receive too little.

Seen through Canadian eyes, the links between the two countries take a very different form. Creating Canada required an act of conscious political will to overcome the strong pull of the United States, and maintaining its uniqueness requires similar determination. It is precisely how much the two peoples share in common that causes Canadians to focus upon, and often exaggerate, the differences between the two countries.

Macdonald and the Fathers of Confederation possessed a vision of what they could create through unity. That vision was given urgency by the fear that failing to act would lead to absorption. What modern politicians have yet to successfully create is the definition of a role for Canada in the continent that moves beyond defending against assimilation and engages its neighbors in working toward common goals.

Canadians' ambivalence about their ties to the United States was captured by a former member of Parliament who once exclaimed, "The Americans are our best friends, whether we like it or not!" The political challenge has been to remain on a similar, parallel track, without converging.

The growing Canadian nationalism of the 1960s and 1970s manifested itself in both in a mounting sense of confidence and in a defensive, protective approach to public policy. The 1967 World's Fair, which coincided with Canada's centennial, let Canadians display their country's achievements. Among Canadians who developed their political sensibilities after the Second World War, it fed a growing sense that they had built something unique and valuable.

Even in the years following the country's hundredth birthday, however, Canadians continued to focus on their relationship with the United States. Thousands of young Americans fled to Canada to avoid the draft, feeding Canadian divisions about involvement in Vietnam. At the political level, Canadian prime minister Pierre Trudeau and U.S. president Richard M. Nixon regarded each other with scarcely veiled contempt. Trudeau's personal relations with American presidents Gerald R. Ford and Jimmy Carter were better, but he remained deeply skeptical of U.S. policy both at home and abroad. For its part, the United States was critical of Canada's unwillingness to contribute more to its own defense and saw the Trudeau government's policies as anti-American and socialistic.[1]

Free Trade and Integration

The Progressive Conservative government of Brian Mulroney in 1984 marked a new phase in the bilateral relationship. Mulroney's election coincided with the rise of conservatism in both the United States and Great Britain, and his personal relationships with those countries' leaders were strong. They liked and respected each other and shared a common philosophy.

The Canada-U.S. Free Trade Agreement, which faced strong opposition within Parliament and among the populace, was a product of the personal relationship between Mulroney and U.S. president Ronald Reagan. It came on January 1, 1989, after months of inconclusive negotiations among officials. It could not have been reached without the mutual trust and confidence of the two leaders.

Mulroney's reelection in 1988 provided the watershed that changed how Canadians regard their border with the United States. It was the last federal election that offered voters a fundamental policy choice about their country's future direction.

The Liberal Party led by John Turner had blocked Senate passage of the agreement and promised to cancel the deal if it won the election. Public opinion polls demonstrated deep divisions on the issue, and Liberal advertisements fed Canadian fears by showing the border being erased. In the end, it was the fact that the Conservatives at least had a plan, and not the substance of the plan itself, that secured their reelection.

The Canadian public accepted free trade, even if it had not welcomed the idea. Public opinion surveys show that free trade grew from having the support of only a minority of Canadians to about 70 percent approval today. The Liberal Party, which was once vehemently opposed, now espouses a range of bilateral and multilateral trade agreements. The nationalist left wing in Canada continued a rearguard action against closer ties with the United States even after Parliament had approved the agreement, but opposition to trade liberalization is marginalized. With the exception of the left-wing New Democratic Party, all parties in Parliament support it.

Free trade was not without cost for Canadians. Removing tariffs left many businesses vulnerable. Inefficient companies—those that competed on price in low-end markets—and those firms that had focused on local markets could not survive international competition. A number of multinational companies closed branch plant operations in Canada, replacing them with increased production runs in U.S. factories.

Other companies and industries flourished, however. The wine industry in British Columbia and Ontario, which had produced wines that were mostly cheap and undistinguished, recognized that they could only survive international competition if they ripped out the old vines and replaced them with vinifera. Canada's wine industry has won increasing numbers of international awards and is more prosperous today than it was before free trade.

The Canadian wine industry's success under free trade provides a model for others. Because high-wage countries

have little hope of surviving free trade by co[...]
price for commodity items, their best opportunity is value-
added niches that do not depend on offering the lowest
price. Many other factors are at play, too, including the weak
Canadian dollar, access to a market more than ten times the
size of Canada's, a strong resource base, and the ability of
Canadian subsidiaries of American multinationals to win
world product mandates for the corporation.

The structural adjustments required by the Canada-U.S.
Free Trade agreement were divisive and often painful. The
transition, however, is mostly complete, and the remaining
businesses do well in a free trade environment. Support for
free trade among business grew as uncompetitive companies closed and the more productive industries flourished.
In Canadian Manufacturers & Exporters' most recent survey of its members, 75 percent supported the North American Free Trade Agreement (NAFTA), with only 6 percent
viewing it as a threat to their businesses.[2]

Under free trade, the Canadian and American economies
have become more integrated and are likely to continue as
such. The two countries are each other's best customers.
Measured in Canadian dollars, Canada's exports of goods
to the United States increased from $102 billion to $359 billion between 1989 and 2000. Imports of goods from the
United States were $229 billion in 2000. That same year, over
85 percent of Canada's exports went to the United States.

Canadians now sell more of their goods to the United States than they consume at home. In turn, the United States sends about a quarter of its total exports to its northern neighbor. Canada is the best customer of thirty-eight of the fifty U.S. states.

The United States today does more business across the Ambassador Bridge between Detroit, Michigan, and Windsor, Ontario, than it does with any other country in the world. The builders of the bridge, which opened in 1929, could hardly have contemplated that 27 percent of all the merchandise trade between Canada and the United States would be crossing it by the turn of the century. Reflecting the growth of commercial traffic, particularly in the automotive industry, seven thousand trucks entered the United States across the bridge on a single day in February 2000.

Canada and Mexico

Like so much of Canada's political and economic life, its relationship with Mexico is defined by the overwhelming American presence. Perhaps the greatest commonality between Canada and Mexico has been the fact that each has had to struggle to define what it means to be a neighbor to the world's only remaining superpower. Even several years after the signing of the North American Free Trade Agreement, bilateral relations between Canada and Mexico remain significantly underdeveloped.

For the past decade, however, the two countries have at least become aware that each other exists. Led by the automotive sector, Canadian industry increasingly plans its production and sales strategies for an integrated North American market. To Canadian business, Mexico is a significant and growing potential market, a manufacturing base, and an entry point into South America. Multinationals rationalize their production throughout North America, locating plants where they can offer the greatest economic advantage, which has made Mexico a more attractive location for manufacturing since 1994. Canadian labor unions, which led the opposition to NAFTA, remain concerned about job losses to Mexico because of wage differentials and the access NAFTA provides Mexico to the U.S. market.

Most Canadians have little firsthand knowledge of Mexico. The Mexican Seasonal Agricultural Workers Program allows temporary Mexican workers to supplement seasonal shortages in Canada. Eight thousand workers took advantage of the program in 2000. Mexican permanent immigration to Canada is low, with only 1,390 Mexicans migrating to Canada in 1998. While a million Canadians travel to Mexico annually, and about 160,000 Mexicans visit Canada, Canadians' opinions of Mexico are still most often shaped by the U.S. media.

Canada in North America

Since NAFTA came into effect in January 1994, two-way trade flows between Canada and Mexico have expanded by 152 percent, although each country's commerce with the United States dwarfs total trade between the two countries. Mexico is Canada's seventh largest export market, while Canada is Mexico's second largest.

Bilateral issues between the United States and Mexico, such as immigration and Mexican trucks on American roads, have not been major factors in Canada's relationship with Mexico. As Mexico and the United States resolve these issues, Canadian concerns are likely to be answered at the same time.

Because of Canada's export focus on the United States, the Mexican market is still underdeveloped. Ottawa has identified ten priority sectors for Canadian trade and investment in Mexico: oil and gas; electric power; mining; information and communications technologies; housing; agriculture and agrifood; environmental equipment and services; pharmaceuticals and biotechnology; medical products and health care; and automotive parts and services.

Cultural and political relationships between Mexico and Canada are also on a very different scale from either country's interaction with the United States. Spanish is not widely spoken in Canada, and the 1996 census recorded fewer than 120,000 people out of a population of over 28 million as claiming Latin, Central, or South American origins. While both countries are members of the Organization of American States and support the Free Trade Area of the Americas, they do not share close military or diplomatic links.

Canada's relationships with its two continental partners are in different stages of development. Canada is closely linked to the United States by geography, history, economics, and culture, and the integration of the two economies is growing rapidly. In contrast, Canadian ties with Mexico are largely economic and, while they have expanded well beyond their low base before 1994, they remain far from mature today. The lack of a shared history—the fact that culturally, diplomatically, and militarily the two nations have engaged each other only on the margins of their relations with other countries—makes converting their separate relations with the United States into a North American Community so difficult.

The Impact of September 11

While ordinary times allow side issues to assume greater importance, crises test relationships and reveal their fundamentals. Despite the irritants that complicate the relationship, Canadians' attitudes toward the United States are positive. The September 11, 2001, terrorist attacks provided numerous demonstrations of how ordinary Canadians view their southern neighbors. As American airports were closed, international flights to the United States were diverted to Canada, and thousands of stranded Americans were welcomed into Canadian homes and public facilities. American flags were hung outside Canadian homes and inside stores and cars. One hundred thousand Canadians participated in a memorial service on Parliament Hill with only twenty-four hours' notice. Canada rapidly became the third largest contributor to the military effort in Afghanistan, and the Canadian government acted quickly to prevent the country from being used as a staging ground for terrorist acts against the United States, all with strong public support.

The attacks challenged Canadians' complacency about contributing to their own defense. While Canada's contribution in two world wars and in peacekeeping has been both costly and significant, successive governments have equivocated about investing in their country's defense. Most Canadian politicians have appeared to share the view expressed by Senator Raoul Dandurand before the fifth League of Nations Assembly in 1924, when he described Canada as "a fire-proof house, far from inflammable materials." When you have that sense of invulnerability, it becomes tempting to skip paying the insurance premiums.

The attacks demonstrated that no country is too remote or too powerful to escape terrorism. If thousands of American lives could be lost in assaults planned on the far side of the world, Canada was at least as vulnerable a target. In contrast with the traditionally weak support for defense spending, an end-of-year public opinion survey showed that 68 percent of Canadians favored a substantial increase in defense spending, although their priority use for the armed forces remained their traditional peacekeeping role.[3]

After September 11, Canadians focused closely on their bilateral economic relationship with the United States. Immediately following the attacks, American authorities dramatically increased border security. The result was delays of up to eighteen hours in crossing the border. Traffic volumes fell significantly and had yet to recover fully more than four months later.

The threat posed by border disruptions in an economy that exports more of its manufactured goods to the United States than it consumes at home caused Canadians to urgently reexamine how to ensure their access to the American market. Long before September 11, personal and commercial traffic between the two countries had outstripped the border's ability to keep up. In a May 2001 speech, Canada's ambassador quoted estimates that the average nontariff border cost can represent about 5 percent of a given product's final invoice price, while the cost to more trade-sensitive industries can be as high as 10 to 13 percent.[4] With Canada-U.S. trade growing at an average of about 10 percent a year since NAFTA, the old physical and administrative structures could hardly be expected to keep pace with the volume.

The two governments had attempted, both unilaterally and together, to make improvements. Through various pass systems for low-risk individuals and initiatives such as the Canada Customs and Revenue Agency's Customs Self Assessment program, they worked to reduce delays for both people and goods. However, even with these changes, the system failed to keep pace with the dramatic increase in cross-border traffic. From 1980 until the September 11 attacks, American border personnel remained at the same level. On a typical day about half of the lanes into the United States were unstaffed.

The terrorist attacks changed how both the Canadian government and the public view border issues. The potential job and investment losses due to delays underscored the importance of ensuring an open border. The government took sweeping measures to prevent Canada from being used as a staging point for terrorist attacks on the United States, while committing itself to expediting legitimate goods and travelers. In turn, the business community created one of the broadest business coalitions in Canadian history, the Coalition for Secure and Trade-Efficient Borders, composed of more than fifty companies and business associations representing almost all sectors.

The government was slow to present an integrated response. At first, it contradicted its previous advocacy of a joint focus on the countries' perimeters instead of on the 200 million annual crossings between Canada and the United States. However, its actions gained coherence after the appointment of Foreign Minister John Manley to chair a cabinet committee on the matter.

Public support for close coordination with the United States was strong from the outset, as indicated in an Ekos Research Associates poll published on September 27, 2001.[5] Asked if they agreed with the statement, "I don't mind giving up some of our national sovereignty if it increases the overall security of North America," 59 percent indicated support, while 53 percent agreed with the statement, "I support creating a Canada-U.S. security perimeter, even if it means we must effectively accept American security and immigration policies." Another newspaper poll recorded support by about three quarters of respondents for a perimeter approach.[6]

It is still too early to gauge the permanent effects of the September 2001 terrorist attacks, but the immediate impact has been to elevate the importance of the relationship on the agenda of both governments and to draw the two countries more closely together in foreign policy and security issues. Canada's decision to place its troops on the ground in Afghanistan under American operational command would have been considered an unthinkable loss of sovereignty before September 11. But in the context of a continuing war against terrorism, it was welcomed by most commentators as a sign of American recognition that Canada can play a meaningful military role beyond peacekeeping.

Despite the George W. Bush administration's proclaimed goal of eradicating terrorism, it is unlikely to disappear. While the cold war provided a superpower condominium that forced potential combatants to play by agreed-upon rules, deadly ancient religious and ethnic hatreds have surfaced to replace it.

Terrorist violence now represents the primary threat to Western democracies. The decentralized nature of terrorism and the fact that it lacks a structure that can be decisively defeated like conventional armies mean that measures taken to guard against it will have to be both sweeping and permanent.

The awareness that neither country can be economically or physically secure as long as the other is a potential target or staging ground for terrorism is likely to have an effect similar to the threat of attack from the air during the cold war. Canada and the United States developed NORAD as a shared response to the Union of Soviet Socialist Republics (USSR). Countering international terrorism will require coordination across a much broader range of organizations, encouraging the two countries to integrate their planning and to look for ways to work with Mexico. Recent reports suggest that the Pentagon is considering options for creating a North American command that could either broaden the cooperation that exists under NORAD or lead to the creation of a trilateral defense arrangement. Whichever strategy is chosen by American planners will reopen the debate about how closely Canada can work with the United States without paying a high price in its military and foreign policy independence.

How the Canada-U.S. border is managed can either facilitate North American integration or serve as an obstacle to it. For the two countries to enhance both their physical and their economic security, the border must be at once permeable to legitimate goods and travelers and a barrier to illegal movements.

A number of approaches to deal with security have been proposed, with a perimeter strategy being the most common element. While a North American perimeter approach to border security issues is widely considered essential to increased continental trade integration, in the short-term at least, it is not possible to resolve it trilaterally. The issues involving the Canada-U.S. border are significantly different from those involving the U.S.-Mexico border. Improvements should be pursued initially on a Canada-U.S. basis. Implementing a more open border between the United States and Mexico needs to be addressed at its own pace and within the different realities regarding that border.

The Canadian business community has expressed strong support for a bilateral approach to border and security questions. The focus is to remove the pressure from the Canada-U.S. border by improving Canada's ability to ensure security domestically. Using a risk-based border management system, it would enable low-risk people and goods to move efficiently while focusing resources on high-risk travelers and cargo. A shared Canada-U.S. approach would comprise three lines of security: offshore interception, first point of arrival, and the Canada-U.S. border.

By expanding its intelligence capacity and working cooperatively with its international partners, Canada can take steps to stop high-risk travelers from entering the country. People and cargo arriving in Canada, including those passing through on their way to the United States, must be properly assessed and dealt with to ensure, to the extent possible, that they pose no threat to either country. Meanwhile, the Canada-U.S. border can be made smarter by moving as much processing away from the 49th parallel as possible. This approach will ease congestion, improve traffic flows, reduce costs for both government and users, and allow border authorities to concentrate on high-risk movements.

The Idea of North America

Unlike the proposal for a united Europe, there is no compelling vision of North America, which remains more an accident of history than a goal. North Americans may be friendly and interested in each other, but their primary loyalties are to their own countries. Who they are still reflects where they are from.

The three countries have made progress in breaking down the barriers to trade that existed before the Canada-U.S. Free Trade Agreement and NAFTA. Even here, however, as the softwood lumber dispute between the United States and Canada demonstrates, they have gone only part of the way.

Where integration has taken place, the process has been piecemeal and pragmatic. The widespread support for improved cooperation in managing Canada's border with the United States since September 11 reflects that pragmatism. The economic well-being of Canada required it, and Canadians saw little that threatened their sovereignty in the measures proposed to achieve it. However, the goal to date has been limited. No one has argued that the differences that define Canadians and Americans as separate peoples should be eliminated in favor of a single North American identity.

Government policy led public opinion in both the Canada-U.S. Free Trade Agreement and NAFTA. Since then, however, Canadian leadership for North American integration has shifted to the private sector. Economic integration is driving trade policy as corporations rationalize production throughout the continent and increasingly look at the NAFTA area as a single market for their products. Commerce also drives the network of infrastructure—the roads, telecommunications systems, pipelines, and transportation networks that hard-wire the three nations together.

While Canada's trade dependence on the United States is simply a fact that is unlikely to change, the government's trade policy before September 11 was to go broader, not deeper. Diversifying through a Free Trade Area of the Americas and new bilateral agreements, while also working to reduce barriers to Canadian exports at the World Trade Organization, would permit new markets to be developed outside of North America.

Sixty-nine percent of respondents in the most recent Management Issues Survey conducted by Canadian Manufacturers & Exporters saw the Free Trade Area of the Americas as a potential benefit, while only 5 percent considered it a threat.[7] However, the clear priority of most Canadian exporters is to consolidate and build their relationship with the United States, followed by a desire to make NAFTA more effective. Canada's largest trading partner is the United States, and the vast majority of Canadian companies are focused on deepening that relationship. With the world's largest market on their doorstep, most Canadian companies have little incentive to move further afield where, in addition to increased transportation costs, they face a cultural distance that would lead to significant increased costs.

This is new ground for all involved. While the European Union (EU) is sometimes suggested as a model, the geographic, economic, and political realities of North America and the position of the United States not only within the continent, but also throughout the world, undermine its relevance. Despite wide differences in the sizes of European countries' populations and economies, no one country is so dominant that the rest of the continent has to do business with it on its terms. Union among the European nations means genuinely shared sovereignty, and each of the partner countries has accepted from the outset that it could be part of a united Europe only if it were prepared to give up a significant portion of its own autonomy.

The European philosophy of union differs greatly from North America's approach. Increased political integration has been an explicit goal of the European exercise from the outset, while the Canada-U.S. Free Trade Agreement and NAFTA were proposed as a means to increase trade without jeopardizing political independence. Similarly, the Europeans chose to create a range of supranational institutions to bring the countries together, while North Americans have focused on removing obstacles to commerce and not on institution building.

It is important to be clear about what is being contemplated. The Conference Board of Canada defines economic integration in terms of developing closer business links through increased trade, investment and technology transfer, creation of integrated production systems, development of complementary transportation and communications infrastructures, and development of the policies, institutions, and business practices that support these.[8]

Within this context, what are the issues or potential barriers that must be examined, beyond whether sufficient political will exists?

First, it must determined if discussions are to be bilateral or trilateral. The Canada-U.S. Free Trade Agreement was a dramatic step forward on the road to North American integration. It was also instrumental in removing a major structural obstacle for Canadian industry. The greatly increased competition to which it gave rise forced Canadian industry to undergo a painful but ultimately successful process of restructuring.

While the Canada-U.S. Free Trade Agreement was truly revolutionary, the North American Free Trade Agreement did not change the fundamentals of Canada's trading relationship with the United States. Others have made the point that the agreement offers a great deal of untapped potential. From this perspective, and at the risk of being simplistic, it is tempting to define the North American integration ideal in terms of NAFTA-plus, the achievement of a seamless market governed by a single set of rules implemented and administered by the three governments to achieve their common interests in a well-functioning and secure North American economy. While there would inevitably be an impact on the social and political development of the three countries, the strategy would be designed to allow each of the countries to develop in its own way.

NAFTA is solid ground on which to build. However, as was the case with free trade, the complexity of trilateral negotiations and the socioeconomic differences between Canada and the United States and Mexico and the United States require that bilateral discussions in a range of areas take place at the start, with the remaining country to be added in the future.

A common currency is especially problematic. A floating dollar lets Canada even out the impact of market fluctuations on output and employment. This flexibility has been useful to Canada in the past, and the existence of a separate currency is a powerful symbol of Canada's sovereignty. In recent years, however, the Canadian dollar has floated in only one direction: down. In addition, growing numbers of multinational companies in Canada do their internal budgeting using American dollars. Finally, the falling Canadian dollar both masks and encourages poor productivity, discouraging investment in new technologies and allowing inefficient companies to remain competitive.

The successful launch of the euro in 2002 will inevitably increase discussion of the issue. While growing numbers of Canadians see a common currency as either desirable or inevitable, the business community remains divided on the question.

If a common North American currency ever arrives, it is unlikely to look anything like the euro. Member countries using the euro enjoy equal representation in a central bank. The United States will not surrender the most powerful currency in the world for the privilege of North American monetary union. Nor is it likely, given the United States' superior economic strength, that Canada or Mexico would have much voice in setting North American monetary policy, although some would argue that the Bank of Canada could become the thirteenth federal reserve district.

Canada—North American and Sovereign?

Before committing to further formal integration, Canadians must deal with a variety of issues, some of which have little to do with integration itself. Chief among them is their traditional fear of economic, political, and cultural domination.[9]

The most contentious issue by far is sovereignty. Concerns about sovereignty rush to the fore with any proposals for a harmonized foreign policy or a common economic policy, as a common North American currency would require.

Ottawa has yet to define a blueprint for the country's relationship with Mexico that extends beyond economics, and political fears have prevented it from promoting closer cultural, diplomatic, or military alignment with the United States. Without a clear vision for the future of the North

American partnership, Canada must respond to external events and other countries' agendas. It is still undecided about participation in National Missile Defense, and the Canadian dollar's continuing weakness has incited debate about whether adopting the American currency is either desirable or inevitable.

Even the emotionally charged issue of bulk water sales to the United States, once politically impossible to consider, has become a topic for debate, much to Ottawa's dismay. As water shortages south of Canada's border become more acute, the need for a dependable source of fresh water will grow, in the same way as finding a secure source of energy imports has become essential to the U.S. economy.

Just as Canadians have tended to define themselves as a people by what they are not—by focusing almost exclusively on their differences from their southern neighbors—the question of what constitutes integration often elicits a negatively framed response. Instead of defining the parameters of closer ties between Canada, the United States, and Mexico, the Canadian response is generally confined to what the relationship should not be—not a customs or monetary union, not a North American EU, not a junior defense partner, not a fifty-first state.

However, Canada cannot map out future directions solely in terms of where it does not want to go. Canada must decide what it wants to be when it grows up.

CANADA IN NORTH AMERICA

The events of September 11 have challenged American assumptions about the United States' invulnerability to attack. The attacks also have forced Canadians to reexamine whether they can pick and choose when their country will be engaged with its southern neighbor. The post–September 11 border crisis forced immediate decisions about a common strategy of border management. The United States clearly would fortify its perimeter approaches; the issue for Canada was whether it wanted to be inside or outside that perimeter. For the vast majority of Canadians, the decision was straightforward. Hundreds of thousands of Canadian jobs depended upon having access to the U.S. market, and, while Canada was not a primary target for terrorists, it could easily come under attack if it became the weak point in U.S. defenses.

Because the continuing threat of violence against Americans by terrorists or rogue states presents the greatest menace to the United States, U.S. actions to bolster homeland security will be permanent and extensive. Canadians could take a somewhat detached view of plans for National Missile Defense, but the measures needed to deal with terrorists are both more urgent and more wide-ranging.

The need for Canada to decide what role it wants to play in North America has gained urgency since September 11. Without a clear vision of how it wants to engage its neighbors, the country will be forced to react to events, instead of driving them. The Bush administration had demonstrated a tendency toward unilateralism even before the attacks, and it will have little patience with Canadians' indecision about their future.

If Canada does not know what it wants, it is unlikely to get it. When the relationship is determined through a series of disconnected negotiations, the country bargains from weakness. That shortcoming is also reflected in the domestic debate, with opponents scrutinizing every proposal in terms of the cost to Canadian sovereignty, instead of measuring it against the benefits achieved.

The bolder and more rewarding strategy would be to develop a coherent vision of how Canadians can participate fully in a North American Community and to enter the discussions as *demandeur* and not as a reluctant respondent. Each country brings unequal assets to the table, but Canada's successes with NORAD, free trade, and, most recently, the Canada-U.S. border demonstrate that the country can succeed when it knows what it wants and enters into the relationship as a full and willing partner.

North America is a continent in transition. It will be impossible for Canada to sit out the changes, so the wiser policy is to anticipate and direct them.

Canada's relationship with the United States will continue to be the dominant factor in most aspects of its life beyond its borders. Given America's size and strength, this reality would exist even if Canada were more populous, much stronger economically and militarily, and were not so culturally similar to its neighbor. It is particularly true in Canada's case, however, given Canada's geographic isolation from every country except the United States.

Notwithstanding these differences, Canada can bring a wide range of strengths to the table, and it is far from having to simply acquiesce to whatever is demanded of it. Its geography is strategic, and despite political rhetoric in Washington about Canada being a haven for terrorists, it can serve as both a buffer and a partner in protecting against terrorism. It possesses vast resources of energy, water, and minerals. Diplomatically and militarily, it can use its size and history to advantage, going places where the United States cannot. Its values and institutions are similar to its neighbor's, and its behavior in the Persian Gulf War and in Afghanistan demonstrates that it is a reliable partner in crises. Canadians tend to overlook these assets, but they are considerable.

As Cuba and North Korea demonstrate, a lack of involvement with world events is no indication of strength or independence. The ultimate test of a nation's sovereignty is how it exercises it.

Nations that are secure in their sense of who they are do not fear partnerships with other countries. Instead, they embrace them and welcome the opportunity to promote their common interest. Canada's greatest successes—in trade, in war, in diplomacy, and in culture—come from its engagement with the rest of the world. Canadian sovereignty assumes its fullest meaning when Canada sets the course. But when the country lacks vision, it can only follow where others lead. The political challenge is to move beyond defining the country in terms of what it is not and to offer a confident and compelling picture of what Canada's role in the world can be.

Opportunities for Progress

At first glance, North American integration may appear to be a cure for which there is no known disease. The concept lacks the political and philosophical appeal of European integration because the factors driving trilateral integration in North America are mostly economic, with the three countries explicitly avoiding political and cultural union. Nor is a closer relationship needed to protect against further hostilities between old enemies; there is no reason to fear military conflict between any of the countries.

North America will always differ from Europe, where no one country dominates the continent. Whatever form a continental partnership takes, the defining feature will continue to be the massive size and power of the United States. A relationship with the world's only remaining military and economic superpower is, by definition, a marriage of unequals. However, no attempt to create a continental community can succeed unless each country feels it is a full participant and is seen by its partners in that light. The political and cultural differences between countries must be respected, or the price of participating will be too high.

Finding the appropriate balance between autonomy and integration will not be easy, but a properly structured agreement can benefit all three countries. The primary driver will continue to be economic, building upon the success of NAFTA. Even with the dramatic expansion in three-way trade since the agreement came into effect, the potential for growth is still untapped.

A new round of negotiations can break down barriers that continue to distort investment and trade as well as drive up costs to consumers. Despite participating in the world's most important trading relationship, Canadian business frequently finds itself subjected to obstacles to trade that are more the product of politics than economics. Unfinished issues from the FTA and NAFTA include antidumping, countervailing duties, agriculture, and softwood, among others. Integration cannot move forward without mechanisms both parties will consider impartial and fair. The political and economic dominance of the United States, combined with interjurisdictional problems within Canada, makes developing such institutions particularly challenging. Given that trade is sometimes easier between Canada and the United States than between Canadian provinces, the scope of this problem is clear. In addition, such institutions must be designed with a view to ultimately including the third partner, Mexico.

Mexico's role requires much closer consideration by Canadians. Mexico has made tremendous progress since NAFTA, expanding economic opportunity and becoming more democratic. It also offers U.S. and Canadian businesses both a growing consumer market and a labor pool that can help make them more competitive. The "great sucking sound" of hundreds of thousands of jobs flooding out of the United States and Canada and into Mexico has not been heard, but Mexico provides a source of affordable labor that can help North American industry be more competitive. In some cases, companies can shift production to North America from Asia or other lower-cost labor markets.

Both the United States and Canada have an interest in reducing poverty and promoting democracy in Mexico. Both countries have invested billions of dollars to achieve these goals throughout the world, and Mexico presents a unique opportunity to demonstrate how trade can be used to achieve important social objectives. Mexico's progress is particularly important as an example to other countries in the hemisphere where democracy remains precarious.

Finally, Mexico offers a gateway for businesses looking to extend their operations into the rest of Latin America. Mexican businesspeople and government officials are sophisticated and experienced in developing international trade. They can serve as a partner in opening up other markets.

Deciding which issues should be dealt with on a bilateral basis and which should be part of a three-country partnership will not be easy. While the objective should be policy coherence throughout the continent, both the nature of the issues involved and the different states of development among the three countries will require movement in the same direction, but at different paces on some issues.

Immigration is one of the areas where flexibility will be needed. The low levels of permanent migration between Canada and Mexico pose few policy concerns. Instead, both Canada and Mexico have issues they need to resolve bilaterally with the United States.

The mobility issues involving the United States and each of its neighbors cannot be avoided. The problem of illegal immigration from Mexico will remain as long as the border stands between millions of Mexicans and a dramatically improved standard of living. Issues between the United States and Canada, including the recognition of credentials and the temporary movement of businesspeople, are less contentious and can all be resolved more readily if the will exists.

While opportunities are available for some degree of harmonization between Canada and the United States, as envisaged in the December 2001 Manley-Ridge agreement, Canadians and their governments will not abdicate control over immigration policy. The skills of immigrants are critical in offsetting Canada's aging population and labor force and in helping Canadian industry overcome growing skill shortages across all sectors. Immigration now accounts for about 75 percent of the growth in the Canadian work force and in ten years will provide all of that growth. Canada needs skilled newcomers, including tradespeople, to remain competitive in international markets. A country's strategy on immigration also reflects its approach to foreign policy, and, while the types of immigrants each country would want to welcome might be similar, neither would be prepared to cede its autonomy.

The fact that the most important immigration issues involve bilateral relationships between Canada or Mexico and the United States should not obscure the larger goal of ensuring labor mobility throughout the continent. If those issues are resolved, three-way harmonization can follow more rapidly. Maximizing economic benefits from NAFTA requires much more than simply eliminating barriers to the exchange of goods among countries. Capital and labor must also be free to move before a truly integrated market can develop. The goal should be to allow business to operate in the most efficient fashion possible, free of unnecessary political constraints.

The growing commercial fusion of North America will continue to drive public policy in a range of areas. Because both capital and talent are mobile, Canadians have become increasingly aware that both corporate and personal tax rates need to be comparable to U.S. rates. As borders become increasingly porous and transportation networks improve, production facilities can be located wherever the tax and regulatory climate is most favorable.

A small but worthwhile first step to building a North American Community would be for the three countries to agree to establish North American lanes at entry points. By giving priority to each other's citizens, the NAFTA partners would signal their determination to forge a closer relationship.

A second initiative could be to develop improved mechanisms for evaluating academic and professional credentials among the three countries. Even within Canada, ensuring labor mobility has been a daunting task, but, as long as no effective mechanism is in place, human talent is wasted and the ability of individuals to relocate in search of opportunity is impeded.

Additional types of nontariff barriers involve differences in standards, whether in health and safety, packaging, electrical standards, emission controls, food testing, or language.

Possible approaches to address this issue include mutual recognition, harmonization, and common policies. While the principle is generally accepted that it is in North Americans' best interests to eliminate these nontariff barriers, the devil is in the details. Even within Canada, it has been a struggle to move toward common policies on these types of barriers.

Bringing many of the regulations that govern business into accord makes good sense, particularly between Canada and the United States where regulatory goals and effects are substantially the same, but the methodology may differ. As they cross their shared border 200 million times each year, Canadians and Americans do not worry that the water they drink, the food they eat, the machines they use, or the pharmaceuticals they consume pose a significant threat to their health and safety. The market is resolving even issues such as bilingual packaging and labeling, which were highly controversial in Canada just thirty years ago. Companies producing consumer goods regularly use English, French, and Spanish on the packaging and in the instructions. The government policy that first mandated bilingual packaging and labeling in Canada generated considerable resentment and resistance both in industry and among English-speaking consumers. In contrast, the market-driven multilingual packaging that is easy to find in any supermarket in Canada or the United States has created no controversy.

The regulation of consumer protection in Canada and the United States is neither inherently better nor worse in one country than in the other. It is simply different, and the differences can be both confusing to consumers and costly for business.[10]

Three key areas for intergovernmental cooperation are developing a shared approach to denying terrorists the ability to enter North America, planning continental trade corridors to speed products to their markets, and protecting the environment. Governments acting in isolation can address none of these issues effectively. By working together to make North America safer, healthier, and more prosperous, the three countries can build a stronger sense of continental community.

A trilateral environmental strategy presents unique challenges and opportunities. While some environmentalists will fear that the slowest partner will always set the pace, creating a race to the bottom, the reasons for developing a North American strategy are compelling. Although trade agreements should be closely focused on commercial issues, building a genuine sense of community must extend far beyond commerce. Pollution knows no national boundaries, and one country's failure to act will inevitably affect its neighbors.

The initiative in constructing a North American partnership need not be confined to government. Business associations in the three countries can develop working relationships to promote common approaches on issues and exchange information about best practices. Universities can create cooperative North American studies programs to deepen the understanding of the continent's history and cultures. Finally, the news media should invest in new bureaus to give their audiences a more balanced and comprehensive view of life in the rest of the continent. While Canadian and Mexican news organizations provide coverage of U.S. events, Canadian coverage of Mexico is skeletal and U.S. outlets have withdrawn most of their Canadian correspondents in recent years.

Building awareness is the critical first step. A more closely integrated North America is inevitable. It will come, either by default, as the forces of technology, commerce, and common security bind the three countries more closely together, or by design, if politicians can create a compelling vision of a North American Community.

For Canada, the worst way to proceed would be as a reluctant and fearful partner, more worried about what it might lose than about what it stands to gain. The test of Canada's political leadership will be whether it can go beyond a narrow and defensive nationalism to a confident assertion of its role in North America.

Canadians demonstrated a pragmatic ability to undergo change both in their acceptance of free trade and in their openness to new policies for security and border management after the terrorist attacks of September 11. Going beyond merely accepting change to desiring it, however, will require leaders with a bold vision and the courage to challenge their country to achieve it.

Notes

1. The *Washington Post*'s former Canadian correspondent offered readers this caustic evaluation:

> Over the years, Canadians might have coalesced around a shared sense of history but for the fact that they have so little of it they consider worth remembering. The country never fought a revolution or a civil war, pioneered no great social or political movement, produced no great world leader and committed no memorable atrocities—as one writer put it, Canada has no Lincolns, no Gettysburgs and no Gettysburg addresses.
>
> For much of the last century, business and political elites in Canada responded to the challenge of building a national identity by cultivating strong anti-Americanism, which manifested itself in protectionist trade and independence on foreign policies.

See Steven Pearlstein, "O Canada! A National Swan Song?" *Washington Post*, September 5, 2000, p. A1.

2. Canadian Manufacturers & Exporters, "2001–2003 Management Issues Survey," September 2001.

3. Jonathon Gatehouse, "In Search of Our Role," *Macleans Magazine*, December 31, 2001, pp. 28–30.

4. Michael Kergin, "The Canada-U.S. Border: Moving to the Fast Lane," speech to the American Association of Exporters & Importers, New York, May 21, 2001.

5. Ekos Research Associates, "Security, Sovereignty, and Continentalism: Canadian Perspectives on September 11," poll conducted for the *Toronto Star*, the Canadian Broadcasting Corporation, and *La Presse*, September 27, 2001.

6. Ipsos-Reid, "Majority (85%) Support Making Changes to Create a Joint North American Security Perimeter," poll conducted for the *Globe and Mail* and CTV, September 30, 2001.

7. Canadian Manufacturers & Exporters, "2001–2003 Management Issues Survey."

8. Conference Board of Canada, *Performance and Potential 2001–02* (Ottawa, 2001), p. 58.

9. The first challenge may be to avoid stepping on linguistic landmines. While proponents may use the term *integration* to describe partnership and cooperation among the three countries, many Canadians consider it a synonym for *assimilation*. Two weeks before the September 11, 2001, attacks, the Liberal Party's pollster warned the government to avoid red-flag words such as *integration* and *harmonization*. See Juliet O'Neill, with files from Janet Hunter, "Integration Talk with U.S. Risky: Pollster," *Ottawa Citizen*, August 24, 2001, p. A1.

10. An example of how regulation can drive up the cost of doing business across borders is the need to conduct separate inspections of deodorants and lipstick with sunscreen imported into Canada on the grounds that these goods have medical properties. In the end, costs to business are passed along to consumers.

3

INTEGRATING NORTH AMERICA
A Mexican Perspective

ANDRÉS ROZENTAL

When Mexican president-elect Vicente Fox traveled to the United States and Canada shortly after his unprecedented victory at the polls in July 2000, he brought with him a courageous proposal to the other two members of the North American Free Trade Agreement (NAFTA): After seven years under a free trade agreement, it was time to set the longer-term goal of creating a North American Community. Only by putting forward such an audacious vision, Fox argued, could governments and people in all three countries work toward a fixed objective. Even if it were to take several decades, moving steadily toward such a target would ensure that the goal would eventually be reached. Although his unorthodox suggestion was met with both skepticism and a certain degree of disdain by traditional foreign policy establishments in Washington, D.C., Ottawa, and Mexico

City, Fox set the agenda for a discussion that now occupies policy planners, academics, and public opinionmakers in all three countries.

Whereas preceding Mexican administrations had often been on the defensive regarding some of the ideas surrounding a NAFTA-plus agenda, the newly elected National Action Party leadership decided that it was time to seize the initiative and publicly present the proposal for a North American Community along the lines of the European model. This change of tactics was disconcerting both to Mexicans and their neighbors because it marked the first time that an initiative of this importance had not been consulted on before its public manifestation.

Nevertheless, Fox's idea struck a chord with much of the media and among think tanks in the United States and Canada. A president of Mexico had managed what many had believed impossible—to unseat the Institutional Revolutionary Party from power and put an end to seventy-one years of hegemonic rule. This in turn led policymakers in the rest of North America to give attention and a higher priority to the new administration in Mexico City.

A few months after Fox's inauguration, during the Quebec City Summit of the Americas, the leaders of Mexico, the United States, and Canada signed a declaration that, among other things, calls for a further consolidation in the integration process. This would be achieved both by fully implementing and strengthening NAFTA and by exploring new avenues of cooperation that the three nations might adopt to take advantage of the enormous, but as yet unrealized, potential of the North American region. The leaders also referred to the need for nurturing the notion of a North American "community" within their respective societies, as well as for generating new ideas on how to further the trilateral relationship and strengthen the association initiated by NAFTA.

In calling for a North American Community, the leaders took what in effect was a first step toward moving the North American Free Trade Agreement beyond its trade-specific agenda and opening the door for a discussion on NAFTA-plus issues such as migration, energy, common security, and a possible common currency. Considering that, even after eight years of success as a trade and investment promoting mechanism, NAFTA still does not have a strong constituency in any of the three countries, the political decision to advance the discussion beyond trade and economic issues represents an important change in policy and a move forward.

Between Quebec and the terrorist attacks of September 11, 2001, some progress was made in identifying the priority issues for discussion within the NAFTA-plus agenda. Initial trilateral meetings were held on energy, migration, and border policy, while both Canada and Mexico's bilateral agenda with the United States continued as before.

In responding to the commitment undertaken in Quebec, the Mexican government has established a working group within the federal system to begin reflecting on how other international experiences with integration could be useful in identifying objectives and alternative instruments for a parallel, ongoing process in North America. Certain key elements have been identified in approaching the goal of moving from a free trade agreement to a true North American Community. The experiences of the European Union, Mercosur, the Association of Southeast Asian Nations (ASEAN), and other successful—as well as less successful—integration schemes have served as guideposts for choosing those elements of a regional proposal that might be applicable to the North American case.

While NAFTA has been a clear success in facilitating and integrating economic exchange among the three partners, from Mexico's perspective it still has not achieved one of its principal goals: to have the benefits of free trade reach all regions and sectors of the country and contribute in a major way to the nation's development process. Although several macroeconomic indicators have gradually converged, the process has been slow and weak, and it shows little sign of contributing significantly or quickly to the upward harmonization of Mexico's economy or society. In some cases, such as the development and use of technology, the gap has even widened further. Real social sector spending by the Mexican government has stagnated, leading to little direct input by expanded trade toward improving education, health, or housing. Most of NAFTA's benefits have accrued to a small segment of the country's economy and to an even smaller number of primarily multinational firms.

When comparing, for example, similar convergence variables among the three NAFTA countries as were applied to Spain in its accession process to the European Union, only gross domestic product (GDP) per capita and Mexico's demographic profile are converging toward its two other partners, while all others are either constant or show signs of continued divergence.

So for NAFTA to realize its full potential and move the convergence process ahead, something more than just opening borders to trade and reducing tariff barriers needs to be considered. International experience has shown that coordinating economic policies and achieving real progress in opportunities, infrastructure, quality of life, productivity, and life expectancy contribute directly to benefit the lesser developed members of the partnership and create opportunities for more effective participation in the overall scheme.

Mexico has to be prepared to take on the overriding objective of convergence for the United States and Canada in turn to share some of the costs required to help the weaker member structurally complete the transformation of its economic and social model. While similarities in many areas exist or have been created over the last few years, formidable challenges remain to laying the foundations for true convergence, especially when assessing the huge costs involved, and to resolving the remaining differences in the rule of law, transparency, levels of corruption, bureaucracy, and so on.

Nevertheless, the fact that much remains to be done should not be discouraging. Europe began its integration progress half a century ago with a very modest agreement to take advantage of synergies in the coal and steel industries. With the 2002 introduction of a common currency (the euro), Europe has taken one more step on the road to integration. For North America, the challenge is to begin a similar process by adding the concept of partnership to existing agreements and by recognizing that, although much still divides the three countries, major identities of purpose and structure provide a solid foundation for a future edifice. All three countries are in a favorable position to build a North American Community. All that needs to be done is for the fact to be recognized, to set the goal, and to proceed with the additional areas of negotiation that will lead to the agreements needed to reach the objective.

As Robert A. Pastor has rightly pointed out in his book *Toward a North American Community: Lessons from the Old World for the New*, the lack of any formal institutions within

NAFTA has seriously impeded the three countries' ability to manage or solve problems before they become crises. Whereas the European Union suffers from an apparent excess of institutions, North America has none. Therefore the first issue to examine is whether the time is now ripe for an institutional framework and, if so, what might it look like.

In its eight years of existence, NAFTA has been characterized by at most a bilateral management of issues and problems, or even a unilateral approach in the case of the United States, instead of a trilateral or subregional approach. This has meant that Mexico and Canada have both been limited to dealing with the United States on an individual basis, while Washington has preferred to keep separate and distinct bilateral links with its two neighbors. The result has been to neglect the North American perspective while favoring domestic or bilateral visions that do not necessarily promote the larger objective of integration.

With the exception of dispute settlement provisions and NAFTA environmental and labor side agreements, the existing North American structure was built solely on international legal texts—often subject to differing interpretations—and the continuing political will of all three governments to make it work. And until now, one could reasonably claim that this has been sufficient. Although major disputes remain and new ones have arisen, by and large the provisions for solving them have functioned well.

Periodic meetings of government officials, who accelerate the tariff dismantling timetable and strengthen cooperation at the operational level, have so far represented
the only mechanism available to the three countries to deal
with NAFTA's day-to-day problems and expand on some
of the basic bargains reached in the initial negotiations.
Only in the dispute settlement area, however, has a post-
1994 trilateral agreement been reached to review and
amend a part of the NAFTA text that has turned out to be
less than satisfactory.

Clearly, therefore, if a higher and wider structure is to be
built, institutions are needed within which discussions can
take place and out of which recommendations to governments
can emerge. This is especially the case as the three countries
assess the feasibility of common migration policies, border
development and infrastructure, shared natural resources,
environmental protection, economic and social policy coordination, and political dialogue on issues of common concern. For these objectives, occasional meetings at the working group level or even ministerial get-togethers are
insufficient. More than the ongoing academic or think tank
debate is needed to creatively invent, propose, and execute
the new dimensions of a partnership for prosperity.

If agreement can be reached on overcoming as quickly as
possible the disparities among the three economies by proposing common objectives in designing public policies,

adopting joint measures that lead to reducing the development gap in the more backward regions and sectors of society, creating the necessary institutional framework for conducting the trilateral relationship, and promoting the convergence of interests and structures to benefit all three economies and societies over the long term, then the region will be well on its way toward having the necessary vision to share a better future. This does not mean that three identical images should be created. Instead what should be pursued is a process to identify commonalities by ratifying traditional principles and by adopting new values and objectives where necessary. In Mexico's case, the greatest challenge lies in consolidating the rule of law in all aspects of the system. The United States and Canada need to channel unilateral or bilateral policymaking into a North American framework designed to benefit all.

Several concrete proposals have been advanced by Pastor and others. At a minimum, a North American commission or coordinating mechanism should be set up to act as a catalyst for reflection, as well as to follow up on decisions reached by politicians. Existing studies and recommendations by the Center for Strategic and International Studies, the Institute for International Economics, the Carnegie Endowment for International Peace, and others contain many useful suggestions on how to develop the institutional framework on trade, energy, migration, development funding, and border security. But what is now needed is a central clearinghouse to assess the political and financial viability of these ideas and make recommendations to the three governments on their new North American agenda.

While the European Commission model is perhaps not what the region needs, Ottawa, Washington, and Mexico City should at least establish a permanent mechanism through which ideas and proposals can be channeled, as well as in which to undertake the complex task of transforming those ideas into action.

One of the areas where immediate progress can be made is in the search for an institutional framework within which to study and make recommendations on development programs for the less-developed sectors and regions in all three countries. Such an institution can be found in the North American Development Bank (NADBANK), but it needs to be modified, expanded, and streamlined. Expansion of the NADBANK—an institution that has functioned well, albeit in a limited way—to channel resources for environmental projects at the U.S.-Mexico border should be one of the short-term priorities in the creation of institutions for North America.

Preliminary agreement has been reached on widening the geographic area at the border within which the bank can fund projects. Its operational mechanism also has been streamlined. But more needs to be done, including bringing Canada into the bank and substantially increasing the range of financing alternatives available for the enormous infrastructure projects yet to be undertaken.

NADBANK could be a first step in creating the North American equivalent of the European cohesion funds that have been—and continue to be—so successful in transferring resources from the richer to the poorer members of the EU and in setting goals for development that meet the needs of the whole community. In turn, Mexico could then be able to adopt specific, Maastricht-type unilateral macroeconomic convergence commitments with the United States and Canada that will be necessary for convergence to take place.

Another area that might be ready for an institutional mechanism is the energy sector. After having unilaterally excluded energy from the original NAFTA negotiations, both Canada and Mexico are today willing to engage in a constructive dialogue with the United States on a common energy strategy. Talks have been held among the three countries' ministers on the subject. North America shares one of the richest and most varied energy resource pools in the world. As each of the three countries advances its domestic energy strategy, identifying synergies and complementarities can be useful in making decisions on how to rationalize and make optimum use of what is available.

Finally, an example of the new agenda that the region needs to address can be found in the aftermath of the September 11 attacks on New York and Washington. Protecting North America and securing its borders has become a major priority in the fight against international terrorism, and there needs to be a common response. Having created a functioning, regional, open trade area, the three countries now need to ensure that the new imperatives of securing borders and territories do not obstruct the legitimate flow of goods, services, and people. The concept of a subregional outer security perimeter could transform internal borders in much the same way as the Schengen agreement did in Europe. In addition, increased effort in identifying and documenting people who live within North America without the knowledge or permission of authorities becomes an imperative. The recasting of the bilateral agenda on migration between Mexico and the United States, which was successfully being pursued before September 11, needs to be reconciled with the newer concept of homeland security. While some would argue that the fight against terrorism is the natural enemy of regularizing migration, others agree that now more than ever the countries of North America need to address the issue trilaterally. A meaningful first step in this respect was taken under the auspices of the Migration Policy Institute, but an institutionalized "trialogue" on these issues is needed as well.

The challenge is clear. Migration, security, energy, labor, and the many other issues on the North American agenda must be discussed, managed, and implemented in appropriate trilateral bodies with the expertise necessary to identify, harmonize, and eventually converge policymaking for the region. This requires an efficient management of the North American relationship and a high degree of communication between and among decisionmakers in all three countries. While the overall agenda and timetable for convergence will have to be set by the leaders of Canada, Mexico, and the United States, the structure and implementation have to be in the hands of operative entities and individuals.

Some of the areas to be considered for the agenda are financial, fiscal, and customs harmonization; informatics; transportation infrastructure; natural resources; and regional development. There are many more, some of which are already the subject of intense efforts at cooperation—for example, organized crime, drug and human trafficking, and the cross-border flow of contraband. The process of identifying problems and creating opportunities for cooperation has yet to begin for other issues.

The key, however, is to marshal the political will to move forward. Mexico has a window of opportunity under the early years of the Fox administration for creating a strategic, long-term partnership with the United States and Canada. The latter have to rise to the occasion and signal their desire to take Mexico up on the challenge. Only with vision and commitment can the North American Community concept work. If policymakers in the three countries make that commitment and pursue the objective, North America—beyond its traditional geographic definition—will become a reality. Although it might take decades for the rules to be drafted and implemented, eventually the convergence process will bring Mexico, the United States, and Canada together into a community of individual nations that combines technology, industry, raw materials, consumers, and other advantages to create the most powerful, single economic entity on earth. This should now be the first priority for North America's political, economic, and social leadership.

4

NAFTA Is Not Enough
Steps toward a North American Community

ROBERT A. PASTOR

More than four hundred million people in 2002 live in the United States, Mexico, and Canada, but few, if any, think of themselves as residents of "North America." The term has described the continent's geography but not its people. The governments of these three countries have devoted so much energy to declaring their differences that they have given their people little reason to consider what they have in common. The nations share a continent, cultures, values, and a trade agreement that has accelerated the pace of social and economic integration. The North American Free Trade Agreement (NAFTA), which came into effect in 1994, could be the foundation on which a North American Community could be built, but much work needs to be done.

NAFTA's purpose was to dismantle trade and investment barriers, and that explains why it reads like a business contract. Although North America is the largest free trade area in the world in terms of population and product, the region lacks a vision of what it could or should become. This may be because some thought NAFTA was already too much for the three nations to absorb, or it could stem from the lack of imagination of the leaders of the three governments or the lack of interest by the people. Whatever the cause, after more than eight years, the question is whether North America should be more than NAFTA.

Bouyant with the legitimacy of having won the first indisputably fair election in Mexico's history, Vicente Fox offered the most ambitious agenda for his country and the entire region. He challenged his two colleagues in the United States and Canada to borrow some lessons from the European Union (EU) and begin to construct a customs union and a common market. Thus far, neither U.S. president George W. Bush nor Canadian prime minister Jean Chrétien have offered much of a response to his proposal. This chapter accepts Fox's premise—that NAFTA is good, but not enough—and it offers options and ideas to flesh out his proposal.

NAFTA's Success and Inadequacies

When it was first proposed, NAFTA was subject to blistering criticism by, among others, Texas billionaire business-

NAFTA IS NOT ENOUGH

man and 1992 independent presidential candidate H. Ross
Perot, who predicted that the United States would lose millions of jobs. As it happened, the onset of NAFTA coincided
with one of the most successful periods of job creation in
American history. The United States did not lose or, for that
matter, gain many jobs because of NAFTA, but the agreement can be considered a success if one judges by its goals.
It reduced trade barriers, and trade and investment more
than doubled in a relatively short time. Today, the first and
second largest markets for U.S. goods in the world are
Canada and Mexico, respectively, and about 85 percent of
both countries' trade is with the United States. Regional integration cannot be measured by the absolute increase in
trade, but rather by the relative increase in intra–North
American trade as a percentage of the three countries' world
trade. Two decades ago, less than one-third of the three
countries' world trade was with each other; today, more than
one-half of their world trade is with each other. A growing
percentage of intra–North American trade is intrafirm and
intra-industry trade. This is a sign that national companies
have become more continental in operations. The 1990s also
witnessed a convergence of values among the peoples in all
three countries and a deepening of social integration because
of immigration.[1]

While NAFTA succeeded in what it was designed to do,
its flaws come from what it omitted. NAFTA was silent on

the income gap among the three countries, and the two gaps, particularly between the United States and Mexico, widened in the 1990s. The Canada-U.S. gross domestic product (GDP) per capita gap widened from $3,400 in 1989 to $7,600 in 2000; the Mexico-U.S. gap went from $15,800 to $26,200 over the same period.[2] NAFTA did not address migration, and illegal migration increased. Until Fox arrived, both the United States and Mexico traded recriminations instead of intelligence about drug traffickers. After the September 11, 2001, terrorist attacks, the United States restricted travel and movement across both borders with little, if any, consultation with its neighbors. Bureaucratic duplication on both borders combined with poorly maintained roads and inadequate border crossings raised transaction costs above the level of the tariffs that were eliminated. NAFTA lacks any serious institutions that could anticipate or respond rapidly to crises, such as Mexico's peso debacle, and it does not offer new plans for integrating the region.

The promise of NAFTA was a new partnership among "three amigos." The reality is that the pattern of U.S. relations with its two neighbors has not changed. NAFTA is not a trilateral partnership. It is a double-bilateral agreement, with the United States dealing with one or the other neighbor, one issue at a time. Highly organized domestic interests—whether sugar, timber, publishing, or telecommunications—have sought to evade NAFTA's rules for competition, and even the most powerful of the three countries has succumbed to those pressures. Integration has benefits and costs, but because of the alchemy of political logic, the costs are more effectively translated into protectionist policies. The only way to change these old habits is to change the structure within which decisions are made—from one based solely on power to one based on rules.

The three countries have reached a level of interdependence in which a shock in one country—such as a financial crisis, a terrorist attack, or the closing of a major border crossing—is felt in at least two of the three countries. However, the three countries have not yet found a way to consult and react together quickly. Integration among the three countries is not irreversible. As opponents to globalization or continentalization seem to grow stronger, it might be hard to maintain the process and levels of integration. Concerted efforts by the governments will be needed to reduce the costs, alleviate the concerns of those who most fear integration, cushion the volatility of external shocks, and narrow the disparities in benefits.

Those are the reasons that the three governments of North America should explore new paths to deepen their relationship. Just three things are lacking: a new vision of a North American Community, leaders who could articulate and promote that vision, and institutions that could channel the spirit into creative and effective policies.

Options

Soon after his election in July 2000, Mexico's new president Vicente Fox challenged his two neighbors to consider a North American common market that would include a fund to reduce disparities between Mexico and its northern neighbors. President Bush cultivated a warm relationship with Fox and offered to help on immigration issues, but even before September 11, he could not find an agreeable formula. Prime Minister Chrétien agreed to a working group on energy, but this has also produced little, and he has ignored the rest of the trilateral agenda. Fox's visionary outline remains unfilled, and the terrorism of September 11 constitutes an additional setback because heightened concerns about security make it much harder for the United States to contemplate the further reduction of barriers on the border.

Regarding the question of whether the three states of North America should integrate in some formal way beyond NAFTA, sovereign states can choose to deepen their relationships in three distinct arenas: security cooperation, economic integration, and political association. Proposals on integration sometimes confuse these arenas or the options within each.

In part because of the acute asymmetry in power, the security relationship—involving cooperation and bilateral security agreements and regional security alliances—among the three governments of North America was relatively stable and cooperative in the twentieth century (with the exception of the period during the Mexican revolution in the century's second decade). Since the Second World War, the United States and Canada have a security treaty on the North American Aerospace Defense Command (NORAD), and both are members of the North Atlantic Treaty Organization (NATO). The United States and Mexico are members of the Rio Pact, the regional collective security agreement in the Americas. The three North American governments are exploring ways to cooperate in the war against terrorism. The United States is in the process of redefining its concept and operations of homeland security. The pivotal question will be whether the U.S. military planners will consult in a genuine fashion with their Mexican and Canadian counterparts with the objective of defining and defending "North American security" in a manner that would reflect the interests of all three countries.

In mid-April 2002, U.S. secretary of defense Donald Rumsfeld established a new Northern Command (NORTHCOM), headquartered in Colorado Springs and led by a U.S. Air Force general. NORTHCOM is responsible for all U.S. military forces engaged in homeland defense, and it will coodinate with the Canadian and Mexican militaries. Canadian and Mexican officials were informed of U.S. plans, but no real effort was made to structure a three-sided organization.

Four tiers of institutional economic cooperation exist among sovereign states: free trade area (FTA), customs union, common market, and economic and monetary union. An FTA is an area where the barriers to trade and investment are dismantled, and goods and services can be traded freely. NAFTA is a free trade area that incorporates some new features, including a dispute settlement mechanism and agreements on intellectual property rights, services, and so on. A customs union is a free trade area with a common external tariff. A common market is a customs union in which labor can also move freely. An economic and monetary union is a common market in which all of the countries use the same currency, have the same monetary system, and coordinate macroeconomic policies.

By proposing a common market, Fox leaped over a difficult but essential intermediate stage, a customs union. In some ways, it is fortunate that Mexico, the country that would have the most difficulty adjusting to the lowest common tariffs, was the one whose president has proposed it. A customs union would dismantle the cumbersome rules of origin, and border inspections of goods would be eased and eventually eliminated. In effect, a customs union would permit the three countries to move to a periphery-based system of security and customs inspection. But that would not be easy to do. Mexico has negotiated many third-party free trade agreements, including one with the European Union, and these will complicate any negotiations for a customs union.

A common market permits the free movement of labor, but this is not a feasible idea for North America for the forseeable future. The United States and Canada are labor-importing countries with the most liberal immigration and refugee policies in the world. Mexico is a labor-exporting country. Given the relative parity in income, the United States and Canada might be able to negotiate a common immigration and refugee policy over a period of years, but the migration agenda between the United States and Mexico is of a completely different order. In a survey, 70 percent of Mexicans—or the equivalent of 70 million people—said that they would immigrate to the United States if they were permitted and thought they would benefit economically.[3] No one expects that many people would leave, but if just 15 million people—double the number of illegal migrants living in the United States today—departed, the consequences would be devastating to both countries. Remittances to Mexico would increase dramatically, but so, too, would the percentage of the population dependent on them. With an open border, Mexico could become the first absentee welfare state. The effect on the United States would be more complicated. Affluent and middle-class Americans would benefit from cheaper labor. Wages for the native-born lower class would drop sharply—as occurred in the 1990s by 7.2 percent—and unemployment among this group would increase.[4]

Even if there were hints of a serious relaxation of the border in the years ahead, that could affect the Mexican national psychology in deleterious ways. People would spend more time planning to leave Mexico than working to invest there. As long as the ratio of wages between the United States and Mexico ranges from 4:1 to 30:1, the incentives to migrate will be compelling. In brief, a common market is an unrealistic and unproductive option until the income gap begins to narrow.

While Europe moved in deliberate stages from a free trade area to a union, North America could skip a stage or borrow ideas—such as a unified currency—from a more advanced stage. As the three economies become more integrated, major shifts in foreign exchange rates have a huge impact on trade and on domestic businesses. Insofar as exchange rates are fundamentally undervalued, they could lead to unwarranted industrial restructuring or they could aggravate protectionism. Both Mexican and Canadian businesses are using the dollar more, and the obvious question is whether North America will move toward de facto "dollarization" or make a formal decision to permit Mexico and Canada to influence U.S. monetary policy.

NAFTA Is Not Enough

Public opinion surveys show that Mexicans and Canadians are ambivalent or opposed to adopting the American dollar, but they are more willing to consider using a different but unified currency, such as the Amero, proposed by Herbert Grubel.[5] The Amero would be equivalent of the American dollar, and the two other currencies would be exchanged at the rate in which they are then traded for the U.S. dollar. In other words, at the outset, the wealth of all three countries would be unchanged, and the power to manage the currency would be roughly proportional to the existing wealth.

States can associate politically with each other in numerous ways. They can coordinate their policies, establish formal procedures to harmonize policies, and establish formal institutions to negotiate unified policies and procedures or to settle disputes. States can also set up new intergovernmental organizations (IGOs). Like any international treaty or obligation, IGOs constrain state activities in some ways, but conventional attributions of sovereignty have not been affected by such associations. In contrast, states could merge with each other in three broadly defined categories: confederation of states, federal union, and unified multinational states.

The confederation of states option corresponds to the Articles of Confederation, the first framework for the U.S. government. Transposed to the three governments of North

America, each would retain most of its existing powers, but they would work together under the auspices of a weak central government to assure the security of the continent.

Two variations on the federal union option are employed by Canada and the United States. The Canadian (U.S.) Constitution delineates the powers of provinces (states) and that of the central government. The Canadian provinces have relatively more power vis-à-vis their central government than is true of American states, but both federal governments have full powers in foreign affairs, international commerce, and national defense. A North American federal union would require that the central governments in Canada and the United States retrieve authority from their provinces and states and then divide power between the union and the three countries.

The unified, multinational state option would eliminate or fundamentally alter the three existing nation-states. The people of North America would elect leaders to a strong central government within a constitution that would assure full respect for different cultures and languages.

The European Union has been considering variations on all three options since the Treaty of Rome in 1957, but the governments have still not selected their preference. If the EU cannot decide after forty-five years, it is unrealistic to expect the three governments of North America to discuss these options seriously, let alone choose one at this stage.

One might expect that the most powerful country would propose, at the minimum, a confederation, but the United States is an unusual superpower. Since the Republican Senate voted against the League of Nations in 1919, a strong element of the party has viewed international organizations and agreements as undesirable restraints on the unilateral actions of the United States. This position has sometimes been confused with isolationism or protectionism, but it is different. It accepts that the United States has important interests in the world that must be defended but views international organizations as anchors that weigh the country down and prevent it from fulfilling its proper role. This unilateral internationalism would be skeptical of, if not fervently opposed to, any efforts that could be interpreted as diminishing its sovereignty or control.

Lessons from the Old World

It is hard to identify a leader in North America, other than Vicente Fox, who is willing to contemplate, let alone propose, a more formal and institutional relationship among the three North American countries. When pressed, some leaders will argue that the people of their country do not want to surrender their sovereignty, but this argument is wrong on two counts. First, surveys in all three countries show the public is willing to consider much more radical changes in North American institutions than their leaders. Secondly, "sovereignty" is so dramatically redefined in each generation in each country that, with hindsight, it appears that the term is deployed as either a disingenuous defense of the status quo or an excuse for a lack of leadership.

Europe has struggled with these questions for nearly fifty years, and its members still have not clearly decided on their destination. NAFTA is only eight years old, and its project from the beginning was much more modest than the EU's. While the three governments of North America are unlikely to step into the debate on long-term goals at the current time, nongovernmental organizations, research institutes, and universities should fill the void with new ideas and old-fashioned cross-border dialogue.

For all these reasons, the most likely path that the three governments are to take is the status quo with modest adjustments. Essentially, the market will decide the region's future with the three governments reacting to specific problems or disputes. This option is both the most likely and the most problematic in the sense that it is least able to cope with either the windfall or the fallout from integration. The business cycle will carry the three economies through periods of growth and decline, but NAFTA will remain oblivious to distributional effects and to the many mistakes or missed opportunities. All three governments could surprise themselves by taking a great leap forward, but this seems possible only if there is a dramatic crisis of some kind.

The differences in origin, membership, governance, and political philosophy between the EU and NAFTA are so great that one might legitimately ask why even consider the EU example. The answer is that it has had more than forty years of experience in integration and considerable success in reducing disparities between rich and poor countries. As one of the central questions of NAFTA is how to integrate Mexico with its two richer neighbors, it would be foolish not to try to learn from Europe's experience. Moreover, by looking at the EU, what is special about NAFTA and what should be avoided or adapted from the EU can be better understood.

Thus far, NAFTA's experience confirms an obvious lesson from the EU—without some compensatory fund, the poor countries experience the most volatility, which serves as a drag on the others. The progress in lifting the poorest four countries of the EU (Greece, Ireland, Portugal, and Spain) has been dramatic. From 1986 to 1999, their per capita GDP rose from 65 percent to 78 percent of the EU average, and emigration slowed markedly. Many studies have tried to explain the success. Four factors were responsible, but no agreement has been reached on the degree to which each deserves credit. The four factors are free trade, foreign investment, the transfer of aid at a level that ranged from 2 to 4 percent of the recipient's GDP, and the countries' economic policies. Much of the money was wasted in many kinds of projects, but the most effective investments were in infrastructure and education.[6]

In understanding what could be adapted and what should be avoided from the European experience, one needs to appreciate the differences between the two integration models. The need for mutual support and community is incorporated in the EU charters, but it is absent from NAFTA. In contrast to Europe, North America's model is more market-driven, resistant to bureaucratic answers, pragmatic, and respectful of national authority. This is the North American advantage, and while an adjustment of NAFTA goals toward a North American Community is desirable, duplicating the EU experience is not a viable option. A new NAFTA preamble would be more effective if it built on the key elements of its own model. North America's leaders are clearly not prepared to adopt one of the political or economic options available, but they are pragmatic enough to understand that some adjustments in NAFTA are needed, and therefore they could borrow ideas from the EU and adapt them. The result could be a deeper North American Community. In general, the new community should build on

—Pragmatism. The deeper North American Community should aim to solve problems, not engage in constitutional debates.

—Markets and rules. All three countries understand the importance of markets to expand the economy and rules to assure a fair negotiating and dispute-settling process.

—Modest institutions. Instead of constructing vast supranational institutions, the North America Community should aim for more modest, lean, and advisory mechanisms.

The first question that the leaders need to face when discussing the elements of a North American Community is whether they prefer a dual-bilateral relationship or a trilateral partnership. The United States has not altered its penchant for unilateralism (for addressing joint problems by itself), and the Canadians and Mexicans still prefer bilateralism (just dealing with the United States). There was a moment at the beginning of the NAFTA negotiations when Canada and Mexico thought they could gang up on the United States, but once they realized that was not productive, they retreated to their old bilateral style.

Dual-bilateralism has three problems. First, the combination of American power and its neighbors' sense of inferiority often leaves a residue of resentment. Second, the issues take a long time to be resolved, if they ever can be. Third, and most important, a broader continental perspective is absent. The leaders deal with one issue, two countries at a time, and therefore rarely, if ever, ask themselves: How can this problem be addressed in a generic way that will benefit the entire region?

Adding a third party to the bilateral disputes increases the chance that they will be decided by rules. That is what a North American Community should do. For example, all three governments are struggling to adjust their agriculture to a competitive marketplace. Most farmers can manage, but the few who cannot compete—such as in timber, corn, and vegetables—use all the legal and political channels to protect themselves. The three countries can continue aggravating each other, and subverting NAFTA, or they could negotiate a North American set of rules that modify the regulatory schemes in the three countries.

If the leaders decide to pursue a trilateral partnership, they must recognize that the weakest link in NAFTA was the lack of credible institutions. Whereas the EU had created too many institutions, NAFTA made the opposite mistake. The three leaders should begin by establishing a North American Commission (NACom). Unlike the sprawling European Commission, which manages and administers European policy, the NACom should be lean and advisory—just fifteen distinguished people, five from each country. Its principal purpose would be to prepare an agenda on North American issues for the three leaders to consider at semiannual summits and then monitor the implementation of the decisions and plans. The NACom would gather statistics from the three governments, and it would commission studies of different sectors, such as transportation, electricity, or technology. These studies would ask what could be done to facilitate economic integration in these sectors on a continental basis, and then, it would submit these analyses with specific options for the prime minister and the two presidents.

A second institution, a North American Parliamentary Group, should emerge from combining the two bilateral legislative groups that the United States has had with Mexico and Canada since 1960.[7] The group would also discuss North American perspectives on issues with which they are dealing.

The third institution should be a Permanent Court on Trade and Investment. The dispute panels established under NAFTA are ad hoc, and recruiting experts who do not have a conflict of interest is proving difficult. The hearings should also be open to the public to build public confidence in the process and in the court's judgment.

Binational commissions of cabinet members have existed in one form or another for more than twenty years. These commissions have never been very effective. That could change if they became trinational and if they responded to agendas prepared by the NACom and approved by the three leaders. To promote a North American perspective, the three governments should also exchange legislative and executive branch personnel for temporary assignments.

Canada and Mexico have long organized their governments to give priority to bilateral issues with the United

States, but the U.S. government has always had a dispersed, episodic approach to dealing with each of its neighbors. This is understandable given the asymmetry in power, but it is not helpful for the conscious construction of a community.

There are two models for reorganizing how the U.S. government addresses North American issues. The State Department model would require a new undersecretary for North American affairs, and the White House model would establish an adviser to the president for North American affairs. The White House person would need to bridge the National Security Council and Domestic Policy Council and chair a cabinet-level Inter-Agency Task Force on North America. President Bush will not be able to translate his personal interest in these issues into effective policy without such a wholesale reorganization.

Institutions are key to structuring the way governments function, but if a North American Community is to emerge, the public also needs a sense of what a North American policy might look like. Transportation is a logical first choice for defining a North American policy, because roads, ships, railroads, and airlines are the arteries that connect the three countries. It is ironic, but true, that the transaction costs of doing business among the three countries have increased above the level of the tariffs that have been eliminated. "Crossing the border," concludes a May 2000 report by a

Canadian member of Parliament, "has actually gotten more difficult over the past five years." The causes are twofold. First, "while continental trade has skyrocketed, the physical infrastructure enabling the movement of these goods has not." Second, the bureaucratic barriers that confront cross-border business make the infrastructure problems seem "minor in comparison."[8]

While some people have been critical of the U.S. Congress for imposing U.S. safety standards on Mexican trucks, the real problem is that there are sixty-four different sets of safety regulations in North America, fifty-one of which are in the United States and twelve in Canada. A NAFTA sub-committee struggled to propose a uniform standard and concluded that "there is no prospect" of accomplishing that.[9] The elected leaders of the three countries should have been embarrassed, and they would have been if anyone had been paying attention.

The North American Commission should review this issue and develop an integrated continental plan for transportation and infrastructure. First, each country should harmonize its own standards on weight, safety, and configuration of trucking and then negotiate a single set of North American standards (with some variations based on weather and terrain). Second, the governments should eliminate "cabotage" restrictions and the "drayage" system, which are notorious featherbedding schemes. Third, the governments should plan and finance new highway corridors on the Pacific Coast and into Mexico. Fourth, the regulatory agencies should negotiate a plan that would permit mergers of the railroads and development of high-speed rail corridors.

At the heart of a free trade regime is the integration dilemma. The reduction of trade and investment barriers also facilitates the flow of illegal goods, and conversely, efforts to prevent smuggling impede the legal flow and, when conducted unilaterally, can enrage the government on the other side of the border. This inherent dilemma was compounded by the extra security precautions that followed the September 11 attacks. There is no simple way to resolve this problem in the short term, but it can be managed better and in ways that make the three governments partners, not angry neighbors. The duplication of documents that comes with crossing the border could be simplified and reduced by half by establishing a single North American Customs and Immigration Service. This agency would be composed of officials from the three governments, trained together in a professional school. The service should be used on both the internal (U.S.-Canada, U.S.-Mexico) and the external peripheral borders.

The United States and Canada have been experimenting with a number of procedures and devices to expedite commerce across the border, and a trilateral approach would permit these to be used with Mexico. Intelligent Transportation Systems rely on transponders to relay information from trucks to customs officials. Staging facilities and pre-arrival systems located ten miles before the border could also reduce delays.

The U.S. government reaction to September 11 panicked Canadian business. While businesses in both countries were concentrating on ways to facilitate movement across the border, all of a sudden, the U.S. government stopped all traffic. With exports to the United States constituting more than one-third of its GDP, Canada's economy shook, and Canadian businesses and trade associations immediately established a Coalition for Secure and Trade-Efficient Borders. They issued two reports, which then became the basis of negotiations between the U.S. and Canadian governments. On December 12, 2001, Tom Ridge, the director of the Office of Homeland Security in the United States, and John Manley, Canada's minister of foreign affairs and chairman of the Ad Hoc Cabinet Committee on Public Security and Anti-Terrorism, signed a Smart Border Declaration. The two governments pledged to provide additional security to the flow of people and goods between the two countries, protection of infrastructure, and new mechanisms for coordinating operations and sharing intelligence. Many of the thirty specific initiatives in the declaration included the procedural devices that had been developed to speed the flow of people or goods. The essence of a new strategy was to distinguish between low- and high-risk flows and to find ways to expedite the movement of low-risk goods and people and to concentrate limited resources on the potentially higher-risk people and goods. It was unfortunate that this exercise was driven by a crisis and was fashioned by only two sides of the three-sided relationship. The United States signed a similar agreement with Mexico several months later, though U.S. and Canadian officials had previously insisted that the two borders were so different that a single agreement was impractical. This dual-bilateral approach will remain the most likely path unless and until different procedures and institutions encourage a genuine trilateral partnership.

Immigration is a different problem on both borders, primarily because of the difference in incomes, but steps could be taken to lay the groundwork for increased convergence of immigration policies between the United States and Canada and reduced divergence between the United States and Mexico.

The only way to significantly reduce immigration to the United States from Mexico is to narrow the wage differentials. That will take considerable time. Even if the Mexican economy were to grow 3 percent a year faster than its two neighbors, Mexico would still need more than twenty years to reach one-half of Canada's GDP per capita and thirty years to reach one-half of that of the United States.

NAFTA IS NOT ENOUGH

In the absence of a demonstrated plan to reduce the gap between Mexico and its northern neighbors, the most likely trajectory will be for that gap to widen and also for the gap between rich and poor regions within Mexico to widen. According to Mexico's economy minister, the northern part of the country has grown ten times faster than the southern part since NAFTA began. A large part of the reason is that the vast majority of foreign investment has gone into the northern states because of poor transportation to the center of the country. At the same time, more than a million Mexicans have moved from the center and south of the country to work in factories before they depart for the United States where they can earn significantly more than on the border. NAFTA, in brief, has unwittingly promoted immigration from central Mexico to the United States while increasing congestion and pollution on the border.

From the lessons learned from the EU, the three governments should establish a North American Development Fund that would concentrate on investing in infrastructure from the border to the center of the country. If roads are built, investors will come and fewer people would emigrate. A second objective should be education. In the mid-1980s, Spain and Portugal had an educational profile comparable to Mexico's, but an infusion of EU funds into higher education had a profound effect, more than doubling enrollment. In contrast, Mexico's level of tertiary education has remained the same. The additional benefit of supporting higher education in remote areas is that these new institutions could become centers for development, and students and professors could help upgrade elementary and secondary schools in the area. That is what Spain and Portugal did.

Instead of creating a new bureaucracy or modifying the North American Development Bank, which has neither the experience nor the mandate, the North American Development Fund should be administered by the World Bank and Inter-American Development Bank.

If the United States contributed at the EU level, that would amount to $400 billion. This figure is useful for alerting Americans to the magnitude of the EU commitment and the meagerness of North America's, but no one believes it is possible at the current time. The World Bank has estimated that Mexico needs $20 billion a year for ten years just to upgrade its infrastructure. A development fund that could loan, say, half of that would have a significant impact on Mexico and North America. Fox has proposed that all three governments contribute in proportion to the size of their economies. The United States' contribution would be the largest of the three but could be in callable capital or loan guarantees. It would be roughly comparable to the amount that the United States contributed to the Alliance for Progress forty years ago. Mexicans already buy more per capita from the United States than any other country except

Canada. Stimulating Mexico's growth, therefore, would have a double return on the investment.

The fund could also have a presence in the United States and Canada, perhaps by financing Centers for North American Studies at selected universities. The EU uses relatively small amounts of funds to finance fifteen EU research centers in the United States, and these play a valuable role in educating the American people on the continued importance of its friends in the EU. Centers for North American Studies in each of the three countries could play that role and several others. They could help to nurture an enlargement of identity that would help Americans to think of themselves as part of a larger entity. They could commission research on problems in North America and request policy recommendations on what to do about them.

There are many other sectors (such as energy) or issues (such as a common currency) in need of comprehensive, continental examination. In the light of September 11, more attention should be given to forging common strategies on security at the peripheral borders of North America and devising ways to facilitate traffic across the land borders.

Is a Community Feasible?

A leap forward in North American relations will require leadership and new institutions. Thus far, only President

Fox has been willing to propose such a leap, and none of the three leaders has displayed the will or the leadership that would make such a plan possible. This may be because subterranean fears lurk in all three countries—Canada and Mexico fear U.S. influence; the U.S. fears immigrants from Mexico and terrorists entering from Canada. Or, at least, that is the conventional wisdom.

Public opinion surveys in all three countries suggest that the conventional wisdom is wrong. All three peoples not only like each other more than the parochial skeptics would have them believe, but they are also more like each other. A majority of citizens in all three countries is prepared to join a larger North American entity if they thought doing so would improve their standard of living and environment and not threaten their culture. Canadians and Mexicans do not want to be incorporated into the United States, but they are willing to become part of a single country of North America under these conditions. A poll of Canadians in late September 2001 found that 53 percent supported the creation of a security perimeter around Canada and the United States and that 59 percent said they would not mind "giving up some of our national sovereignty if it increased overall security in North America."[10] The leaders in the three governments, however, are far behind the public. While government officials zealously guard obsolete conceptions of sovereignty, the people pragmatically ask:

Can our lives be improved by experimenting with a different approach?

At Vicente Fox's ranch in Guanajuato on February 16, 2001, Fox and Bush agreed to consult with Canada and "strive to consolidate a North American economic community whose benefits reach the lesser-developed areas of the region and extend to the most vulnerable social groups in our countries." In the absence of any ideas or progress toward this goal, Fox and Bush reaffirmed at the conclusion of Fox's state visit to Washington, D.C., on September 6, 2001, the "importance of vigorous measures to ensure that the full benefits of economic development and trade are extended to all regions of Mexico." They set up still another working group. The words and sentiments are right, but the policies and the resources do not follow. At a summit meeting in Monterrey, Mexico, in late March 2002, Presidents Fox and Bush announced a "Public-Private Partnership for Prosperity" and pledged $30 million for many small projects under its auspices.

The proposal sketched in this paper for a North American Community is substantial, not symbolic like the Monterrey initiative. It also is very different from what was contemplated or implemented in Europe, except that it builds from a similar premise that all the nations of the region need to help each other or they will find themselves harmed by their interdependence. The North American

Community requires some modest and lean institutions to help the leaders of the three governments think continentally, fashion new plans to facilitate economic integration, and reassure people about social integration. None of this is possible unless concerted steps are taken to reduce the income gap between Mexico and its neighbors and unless the two bilateral relationships based on power are transformed into a trilateral one based on rules. If Mexico could sustain a rate of growth that is twice that of the United States, and if it altered the implicit NAFTA development strategy, then one would see progress and the psychology of Mexicans and of North Americans would change. Mexico would be viewed as a partner, and the prospects of building a community would grow.

Notes

1. See Ronald Inglehart, Neil Nevitte, and Miguel Bazañez, *The North American Trajectory: Cultural, Economic, and Political Ties among the United States, Canada, and Mexico* (New York: Aldine de Gruyter, 1996); and Robert A. Pastor, *Toward a North American Community: Lessons from the Old World for the New* (Washington: Institute for International Economics, 2001), pp. 81–83, 156–164.

2. Conference Board of Canada, *Performance and Potential, 2001–02* (Ottawa, 2001), p. 3.

3. Pastor, *Toward a North American Community*, p. 125.

4. Ibid., p. 127.

5. Herbert Grubel, *The Case for the Amero: The Economics and Politics of a North American Monetary Union* (Vancouver: Simon Fraser Insti-

tute, 1999). An October 2001 survey in Canada found that 55 percent favored the same currency as the United States, but 59 percent opposed adopting the U.S. dollar. See Allison Dunfield, "Canadians Feel Closer to the U.S., But Reject Currency," *Globe and Mail*, November 6, 2001.

6. For a detailed analysis of these studies, see Pastor, *Toward a North American Community*, chapters 2 and 3.

7. For a fuller development of this idea, see Robert A. Pastor and Rafael Fernandez de Castro, eds., *The Controversial Pivot: The U.S. Congress and North America* (Brookings, 1998).

8. Val Meredith, M.P., *Trade Corridors: A Report to the Canada-U.S. Inter-Parliamentary Group* (Ottawa: House of Commons, May 2000), pp. 7–8, 10–11.

9. NAFTA Land Transportation Standards Subcommittee, Working Group 2, *Harmonization of Vehicle Weight and Dimension Regulations within the NAFTA Partnership* (October 1977), p. 2.

10. The poll was conducted by the Ekos Research Organization for the *Toronto Star* and CBS News. It is cited by Barbara Crosette, "Support for U.S. Security Plans Is Quietly Voiced across Canada," *New York Times*, October 1, 2002.

CONTRIBUTORS

PERRIN BEATTY is president and CEO of Canadian Manufacturers & Exporters.

PETER HAKIM is president of the Inter-American Dialogue.

ROBERT E. LITAN is vice president and director of Economic Studies at the Brookings Institution, where he holds the Cabot Family Chair in Economics.

ROBERT A. PASTOR is vice president of international affairs at American University and director of the Center for North American Studies.

ANDRÉS ROZENTAL is president of Consejo Mexicano de Asuntos Internacionales.

INDEX

93–94; natural resources, 15,
27; need for rule of law, 81;
oil industry, 15; relations
with Canada, 40–43, 56, 85;
relations with United States,
8, 85, 92, 105–06; security
cooperation with United
States and Canada, 48–49;
social spending, 76–77;
sovereignty concerns, 26–27;
trade with Canada, 5, 41, 42;
trade with United States, 4–5,
89; trucking industry, 9, 107;
wage levels, 23–25, 41, 96;
working group on
integration, 76
Migration: within European
Union, 17; within Mexico,
111. *See also* Immigration;
Labor mobility
Migration Policy Institute, 84
Military: Canadian, 44, 45, 47–
48, 60, 93–94; Mexican, 93–94;
Northern Command
(NORTHCOM), 93–94. *See
also* Defense; Security
cooperation
Mulroney, Brian, 36–37
Multinational corporations:
benefits of NAFTA, 77, 89;
Canadian subsidiaries, 38, 39;
plant locations, 41
Multinational states, 98

NACom. *See* North American
Commission

NADBANK. *See* North American
Development Bank
NAFTA. *See* North American
Free Trade Agreement
NAFTA-plus proposals, 12, 13–
14, 54–55, 74, 75, 85
National Action Party (Mexico),
74
Nationalism, 26, 35–36
National Missile Defense, 57, 58
National Security Council (U.S.),
106
New Democratic Party
(Canada), 38
News media, 33, 69
Nixon, Richard M., 36
Nontariff barriers, 66–67
NORAD. *See* North American
Aerospace Defense Command
North America: development of
identity, 113; economy, 1–2;
lack of vision of, 50–51, 87,
88, 91, 103. *See also* North
American Community
North American Aerospace
Defense Command (NORAD),
33–34, 48, 59, 93
North American Commission
(NACom), 18, 81–82, 104–05,
107
North American Community:
NAFTA as foundation, 87;
proposals, 2, 73–74, 86, 115–
16. *See also* Future integration
North American Court on Trade
and Investment, 11, 105

Index